"This book is an exem
marriages. Jessica has
and partnered them w
ommend this to anyone who is married or considering marriage. By
far, the best book I've read on the bonds of marriage."

—Bruce A. Rauma, Senior Pastor
WOW Church of the Nazarene

"How do you take a marriage from just surviving to thriving? In
The Divine Marriage, Jessica Rothmeyer draws on her personal life
experiences and extensive work as a counselor to lay out a practical approach to developing a healthy, happy, growing biblical marriage. Every chapter is loaded with examples and insights that will
help your marriage soar to new heights!"

—Greg Pagh, Pastor
Christ Church, Otsego, MN
Chair of BlessMN – Adopt Your Street in Prayer

The
DIVINE
marriage

GOD'S DESIGN
For a *Rewarding*
and Fulfilling Relationship

WISE *Ink*
CREATIVE ★ PUBLISHING

The

DIVINE
marriage

GOD'S DESIGN
For a *Rewarding*
and Fulfilling Relationship

Jessica Rothmeyer Ph.D.

God Bless you
Marriage!

Jessica Rothmeyer

ISBN 13: 978-1-940014-82-1
eISBN 13: 978-1-940014-83-8

Library of Congress Catalog Number: 2015951135
Printed in the United States of America
First Printing: 2015
20   19   18   17   16   5   4   3   2   1

Cover design by Jess Morphew

Wise Ink Creative Publishing
837 Glenwood Ave.
Minneapolis, MN 55405
www.wiseinkpub.com

To order, visit www.itascabooks.com or call 1-800-901-3480.
Reseller discounts available.

*I would like to dedicate this book to the revival and
resurrection of Godly marriages in this world.
I pray that these marriages lead individuals, families,
and whole communities to renewed hope, faith, and joy.*

Introduction

My greatest hope in writing this book is that readers will experience the blessings and fulfillment that come from living out a Godly marriage. There is no greater purpose or pleasure in marriage than knowing that you are functioning according to God's design. My passion and purpose in life is teaching others how to have a biblical marriage and teaching couples how to be effective in God's kingdom **together**.

My personal experiences as well as my work as a counselor inspired me to write this book. For the first four years of my counseling career, I provided in-home family counseling to blended families (divorced, remarried, adopted, and foster) and for juvenile probation/child protection cases. I spent the next seven years working in a clinical counseling setting and worked mostly with individuals diagnosed with depression, anxiety, and co-occurring mental, chemical, and physical health issues. During these years, I learned many valuable lessons as a young counselor as God was using this time to educate and refine me in how to teach and counsel people to seek emotional freedom and spiritual growth. Finally, after a great deal of prayer and divine intervention, I was able to start my own business with my husband, Scott. Our vision for this business was to help our clients find physical, emotional, and spiritual healing through Christ and teach people biblical wisdom to apply to their marriage. As we discussed and prayed about the name of our business, we knew we wanted to give the honor and glory to God. God's advice and direction are always so much better than our own. It was through this process that our business came to life as Divine Revelations Counseling: Divine (of or from God) Revelations (the divine or supernatural disclosure to humans of something relating to human existence or the world) Counseling (assistance or guidance in resolving personal, social, emotional, or spiritual problems and difficulties).

Scott and I had each personally dealt with failed marriages of our own. Through these experiences, God instilled a passion for marriage counseling in both of us. We understood the pitfalls of living outside of God's plan for marriage; we had greater insight into how spouses can lose compassion, love, and forgiveness for one another due to unresolved conflict; and we both grieved for our children, who were most hurt by the brokenness that comes from divorce in a family. Scott and I believe God gave us a clear and concise way to teach couples about how to live out a fulfilling marriage and a spiritual life together, the kind that God would intend for all of us to have. We encourage the couples we counsel to rise above the "typical" marriage and to not settle for just **surviving**. We teach our clients to be the couple that every other person in their church, social circle, and community will take notice of and say, "I want a marriage like theirs."

The chapters in this book will address the core issues that cause couples to become caught in vicious cycles of conflict, unforgiveness, and disconnectedness. It is true, there is a little hard work and sacrifice in making any relationship work, but with better understanding of our natural human instincts, our inborn tendencies, and valuable wisdom from God's Word, it can be quite a bit easier than you think! And your marriage can be mind-blowingly better than you could have ever imagined.

Reading this book as a couple is highly recommended. These concepts will be helpful to discuss and process together, hopefully instigating intimate and healing conversations.

What Is Wrong with Marriages Today?

There are varying statistics about marriage and divorce, but on average 50 to 60 percent of all marriages end in divorce. And, since today many people divorce and remarry, it is important to know that 60 to 70 percent of second marriages also end in divorce. Yikes!

My husband Scott and I have a God-given passion for marriage; seeing and hearing so many people struggle in their marriage breaks our hearts and surely breaks God's heart too. But that is not the end of our grief; after many years of providing marriage counseling, we know that out of the 50 percent of marriages that manage to stay together, the majority are really living miserably and staying together for the kids, financial/emotional security, religious beliefs, or out of pure willpower.

My husband and I want to counsel those couples who have the desire and motivation to be "one-percenters." I define a one-percenter marriage as a couple who inspires everyone around them to say, "Awww, look at those two! They are so in love. They look so happy together. Look how well they treat each other. I want a marriage and relationship like theirs." It is easy to recognize a couple that is truly living a biblical marriage by their love and respect for each other, their ability to serve one another with joy, and their pure contentment with their spouse and their life together. Good news: it is easier than you think to have a marriage like this. It takes a change of mind, a gaining of wisdom, and a commitment to think and behave in ways that are **not simply reactions to your natural instinct.**

For the many couples we have helped, two ideas that have been important to understand are: men and women are created **instinctually** different and were designed this way by God and, secondly, that we are each **individually** born with strengths and weaknesses that are unique to different temperaments which are not gender based. These two components of understanding our identity and roles in a relationship give us insight about what causes problems in communication, conflict, and essentially every area of the marriage.

There are two main ideas in this book that will help couples live out a "Divine Marriage":

1. God created men and women in His image, but we are each, as a male and as a female, only a partial image of God. Therefore, the differences in genders and inborn temperaments begin to cause misunderstandings and conflict within the marriage. Without seeking wisdom or applying new behaviors **outside of our inborn tendencies,** we will foster hurts and wounds that begin to occur within the relationship. These hurts and wounds will possibly lead to emotional distance, low marital satisfaction, and even divorce.

2. To help individuals understand their paths to individual and marital success by applying biblical roles and spiritual wisdom to their lives and relationships. It might seem there are more chapter "themes" directed to men, but a great need exists for men to understand their wives and be comforting in a way that is not instinctual to husbands. Women are naturally more relationship savvy but need redirection and encouragement in the area of learning to be forgiving and submissive/respectful to their husbands.

Here is our initial prayer for you:

Father in Heaven,
*Please bless this man/woman/couple as they read this book. Let it be a personal and intimate revelation to them, from You, about the abundant gifts and blessings that are found in a healthy and Godly marriage. Allow the truths and wisdom found in each chapter to weave their way into their hearts, minds and souls. Help them, Lord, to let down their guard, forgive themselves, and forgive their spouse for hurts and wounds in the past. Due to our human nature, we **have** and **will** continue to hurt those that we love without Your wisdom and Your intervention. Father, help each person to understand the word **grace** (unmerited and undeserved favor and love) and have this kind of grace for one another in the marriage. Reveal to each hurting heart how much You love them and how You want to resurrect and bless their marriage. With every marriage saved and every family restored, we promise to give all the Glory to You, Lord Jesus.*
In Jesus's precious and holy name we pray.
Amen.

You are a Unique Creation

"For you formed my inward parts; you knitted me together in my mother's womb. I praise you, for I am fearfully and wonderfully made. Wonderful are your works; my soul knows it very well."
—Psalms 139:13-14

There are many self-help marriage and relationship books that address the differences between a husband and a wife; I believe this book is different in the ways it explains how men and women can understand and accept those differences and how to apply wisdom in these areas, so they can enjoy the blessed and fulfilling marital relationship God intended for all of us to have.

This chapter will address our identity. Understanding our identity is necessary as we begin to talk about the significance of God-given gender traits and roles. Our identity is comprised of so much more than a title, a single strength, or even our role. If you were to enter into therapy to address identity issues or self-esteem, many counselors would focus on who you are in the family (mother, brother, daughter), what job title you have, or what natural talents you have (creativity, intelligence, athleticism) in order to help you gain a sense of your identity. But what happens when we only "hold on to" the fact that we are a mother, a father, a chef, or a firefighter? What happens when our children leave home or we retire? What if through uncontrollable circumstances we fail at these particular roles? Does that mean that our lives are worthless and we have no identity?

As a Christian, a magnificent and freeing revelation about our identity is that it is not **accomplished** or **earned**. It is given to each of us by a Creator. As the Scripture above explains, we were knitted together in our mothers' wombs. We are not an accident or a random collision of DNA. God took special care in our design, with a very particular purpose and destiny for each individual. Once we grasp this concept, we can begin to explore whom God created us to be in marriage, work, ministry, and parenting and how each of us, individually, needs to surrender to Him for the best possible outcome in our lives.

My husband and I say our lives would never be as good without God, and knowing His guidance, protection, and intention for our lives is significantly better than being on our own. Without God, people are left to find a place in this world, perform, achieve, and gain the acceptance of others for their sense of self or purpose. But understanding your worth through God's eyes means you never have to feel like a failure again. Everything good and valuable about you was **hardwired** within you by God, at birth, and if we just focus on that and make our heart's desire to have a life that is pleasing to God, we will always be a success. If we can actually grasp and accept this to be the truth, there is abundant joy, relief, and peace in this revelation.

How to Find Your Identity

The first step to finding your identity is understanding the instinctual and natural "wirings" that are incorporated into biblical roles as men and women. Everyone must comprehend that we are uniquely and specifically created by God **with a purpose**. These roles and temperament types are somewhat generalized, but they are accurate and **biblical**. There will always be "exceptions" to these roles/rules. Sometimes a spouse's temperament or their role in their family of origin will push them outside of their more natural gender tendencies. Sometimes, due to media, single parenting, or "worldly teachings," we begin to learn we **should** or **need** to take on the roles of the other gender and be comfortable with being both husband and wife. And, most often, if an individual does not seem to identify with who God created them to be in their role as husband or wife, dysfunction within the relationship will set in and they will falsely identify with opposite gender roles. Abuse, past hurts and wounds, or trauma will all begin to pervert or distort the truth about a person's gender role and identity.

God created each of us with a role and a purpose as a man or a woman. God created each of us with a specific temperament that contains natural strengths and weaknesses. Lastly, God gave each of us spiritual gifts that motivate us to serve and help others, which gives purpose and meaning to our lives. All of these components make each human being as unique as a snowflake. No one person is created exactly the same as another, but all people are as valuable and precious to Him.

Please understand you are not bad or unlovable if some of these generalizations do not seem to "fit" you, but I would encourage you to seek the truth of what you believe God's plan and design are for you. Allow your thinking to be challenged. After fifteen years of facilitating marriage counseling, the common themes of gender differences (discussed in the following chapters of this book) are consistently revealed as problematic and unhealthy in marriage. Through the wisdom and healthier thinking unveiled in this book, many of our couples have turned their distant, conflict-filled, and frustrating relationships into thriving, fulfilling, and God-honoring marriages.

A Relationship Myth:
Women Are Crazy and Men Are Stupid

These are two generalized statements about the frustrations couples experience when dealing with the opposite sex in relationships:

1. Men are often left to feel incapable of pleasing their wives and frustrated that a woman can be irrational. Eventually men feel like a failure as a husband; lacking the wisdom or skills to "make her happy" will eventually lead a husband to make a comment similar to: "My wife is just . . . crazy. She is so emotional, and she doesn't take my advice. Her feelings just aren't logical or helpful. She should just stop feeling that way."

2. Most women are perfectly capable of communicating what they need to feel close with their husbands in the marriage, but, alas, women are left feeling let down time after time and view the lack of care from our husbands for our emotional well-being as neglect and rejection. This will lead a wife to make a comment like, "How can my husband not understand my needs? I tell him all the time. Either he is just stupid, or he really doesn't care about me at all."

Of course, neither of these statements is **actually** true; women are not crazy and men are not stupid. These frustrating and hurtful statements are further evidence that our genders create differences in how we interact and react to our spouse in a relationship. We have different instinctual needs, and reacting instinctually to the opposite sex's attempts to get those needs met can be very hurtful and damaging. This damage could be inflicted upon the marital relationship, but it could also be very damaging to the individual, as a person, hitting them at their core. It is a well-known fact: no one can hurt us as deeply as our spouse. This is because we are connected to them on a spiritual, emotional, and soulful level, like no one else on earth.

It is vitally important to understand why we, as different genders, think and act the way we do in relationships and how to treat each other with sincere kindness and respect. One gender role is not better or worse, right or wrong, crazy or stupid . . . simply different from the other.

I, Tarzan. You, Jane.

Believe it or not, caveman days were probably a lot less difficult when it came to conflict and relationships. The roles were easily identified. Men provided food and shelter and protected their family. Women bore and cared for children and made their place of living pleasant and a home. The world we live in today is complicated. We are told from a very young age that we can and should do it all: be all you can be, be strong, be vulnerable, be successful, and, above all, gain the approval of others. What a stressful and anxiety-ridden life we lead! After only a few years of counseling, I realized that the majority of the population was either depressed, anxious, or a combination of both. Very few people seem to have confidence, joy, and peace in their lives. I know, without a doubt, that the more you come to understand your role, your identity, and your purpose, as was designed for you by God, the more you will have all of the positive spiritual benefits that come with such wisdom. The first step is to simplify the roles of husband and wife.

There are several chapters on the deeper, inner workings of both men and women and how these are biblical traits, but here is a brief overview to get us started:

Men:

God designed men to be warriors. They hunt, they provide, they work, and they protect their family and friends with God-given courage. They fight for their country, and they defend their honor. A man requires the respect and support of his loved ones in order to be the healthiest person he can be. Men are logical, compartmental, and solution-oriented in how they think. Men desire to be a victor, gain property, attain achievements, complete goals, and secure their finances. Men need to be allowed to dream and need to be encouraged to go after those dreams. These are all instinctual traits in men and, to some degree or another, a driving force in how they act and react in the marital relationship.

Women:

God designed women to give and receive love. They birth, love, and care for children. Women care for everyone—young and old—in the world. Women are compassionate, serving, sacrificing, and desire to be helpful to and needed by others, especially their husband and children. Women want to make their home nurturing, safe, and enjoyable. Women yearn to have a deep and intimate emotional connection with their husband. All women need to feel precious, appreciated, and cherished above all else in the mind of their husbands, and they require proof of these things through their husbands' words and actions. Every woman's heart is won by a man's pursuit of her, and she will need that pursuit and emotional care to continue for the **rest of her life** in order to feel safe and secure in the relationship. These are all instinctual needs in women and are the driving force in how they act and react in the marital relationship.

I Am More Than Just a Man or a Woman!

Yes, each of us has instinctual tendencies as a male or female, but humans are complex beings, and there **is** more to us than our biblical gender roles. God gave each of us an inborn temperament.

Temperament is the idea that each of us is uniquely created by God with inborn strengths and weaknesses. These are easily identified by a quick and simple assessment. The idea of identifying one's temperament has been around since the days of Aristotle. Assessing and using the results to help people in counseling has been significant for many professionals for forty-plus years. The inventory I use in my counseling business is the ARNO Profiling System created by Drs. Richard and Phyllis Arno.

Temperament analysis is different than a personality test. Your personality has developed based on **your temperament** (core inner wiring), plus the components of: which family you were born into, the amount of stress in your surroundings, trauma or abuse you experienced, and what kind of spiritual environment you were exposed to. All of these ingredients combined start to develop your personality. **Your temperament** consists of your natural inborn strengths and weakness, created and hardwired within you by God for a specific reason and purpose. As we grow in maturity and wisdom, we can learn to compensate for weaknesses and minimize their effects in our lives. If we are wise, we can learn to use our strengths to better ourselves and the world around us.

Nothing about you is a mistake. Learning who you are, both in natural talents and instinctual shortfalls, is essential in having good self-confidence and healthy relationships.

The ARNO Profiling system accurately assesses your social tendencies and the amount of leadership and control you do or do not want in life, as well as how much affection you give and receive. Have you ever been frustrated that you enjoy going out and spending time with friends, but your spouse just wants to stay home all the time? Do you think your spouse tries to be too controlling, which leaves you feeling resentful? Do you have your needs for affection go unmet and wish your spouse could be more physically or verbally affectionate? These are all areas that can be better understood by knowing your and your spouse's temperament. Having the full explanation of one's temperament—along with the acceptance that people are simply wired uniquely by God, not "broken or dysfunctional" in some way—can be life changing, both personally and in your marriage.

The addition of the temperament assessment to my counseling practice has radically changed how Scott and I counsel and has exponentially increased the speed at which our clients are finding healing, self-acceptance, forgiveness, and significant improvement in stress and anxiety within their marriage.

At Divine Revelations, when we begin with a new couple, we start with the importance of fulfilling our biblical roles as husband and wife. God created each of us differently as a sex, **male or female for a specific purpose**. Next, we go over their temperament analysis results to uncover a more in-depth understanding of how they interact with one another and how they are affected by the world around them. Sharing the results of this personal inventory with each other, as spouses, also helps the couple to be more forgiving of the ways they might have been hurt or rejected by their loved ones throughout their relationship. These revelations are helpful to the couple; first, for healing the hurts and wounds created by their differences, and, second, for understanding how those differences caused damage to the marriage. Then, the insight can also extend to healing life-long family, childhood, or past relationship trauma that took place long before the couple was married. The understanding and acceptance of their temperaments adds mercy and compassion for one another by recognizing the spouse or a parent might have struggled to meet their personal needs. This can happen because we all have different temperaments, not because that person had bad intentions or did not try to love or care for you. He or she was simply unaware or incapable of meeting your needs.

For example, my personal temperament is one in which I **give** and **require** a ridiculous amount of affection and approval, literally the highest you can score in both areas. My husband, on the other hand, needs very few signs of affection or approval and **gives** even less affection than he requires. He struggles to give affirmation to others because he does not require it himself. Without this valuable insight about our temperaments, I might begin to feel neglected and unloved by my husband and resent him for rarely meeting my high needs for affection. And without temperament awareness my husband might begin to feel like a failure and frustrated that he is never "giving enough" affection, and he might begin to think I am just too demanding and there is something **wrong with me**. One of the most profound revelations that can come out of discovering your temperament needs: **there is nothing wrong with you**. Your strengths and weaknesses are simply how God designed you to be, and because we are all so uniquely created, it can be difficult to understand and accept the temperament strengths and weaknesses of those different than us: our spouse, children, parents, extended family, or friends. It is fairly normal to assume that everyone thinks or feels the same way we do, but when we observe or experience that they do not, we might say to ourselves, "What is wrong with that person?"

Understanding our identity helps us have more self-confidence and also gives us more accurate insight into how we can build on our strengths and learn to compensate for our weaknesses. Learning to do this for our spouse can be a huge strength in a marriage. We can cheer on our spouse in their strengths, helping them to be more successful in life and within the marital relationship. They will feel encouraged and empowered by the support of their spouse. This technique works for weaknesses as well. Instead of having conflict about the lack of connection due to their temperament differences, the couple can openly, and in a supportive way, discuss how to problem-solve and ask for forgiveness for the ways they might unintentionally hurt one another or fall short due to their instinctual tendencies and reactions. On a personal level, learning to submit our weaknesses to God and ask for His supernatural help, guidance, and inspiration in our areas of weakness will be a lifelong area of spiritual growth. This process encourages us to be dependent on God, which is truly His desire for us. It is an illusion and false belief to think we will ever achieve perfection or anything close to it. We are in constant transformation by the Holy Spirit, and our refining and sanctification happens from the day we give our life to the Lord until the day we join Him again in Heaven.

> "But he said to me, 'My grace is sufficient for you, for my power is made perfect in weakness.' Therefore I will boast all the more gladly of my weaknesses, so that the power of Christ may rest upon me."
> —2 Corinthians 12:9

This means it is necessary to learn and identify the temperament differences that will inevitably cause conflict in the marriage. Recognizing how the differences in each other's temperaments require you as a couple to put effort into meeting each other's needs in ways that are different than your own and probably outside of your natural talents. We must reach above and beyond our natural tendencies, at times, in order to be a good husband or wife. See how helpful it is in this respect to have the supernatural help of God in these endeavors?

We have spent many sessions with our counseling couples on this exact issue of attaining wisdom-based skills, and I will be offering specific techniques in the future chapters of this book in how to execute these skills: how to operate outside of our natural talents and tendencies. Without wisdom about what your spouse's physical, emotional, and spiritual needs are, we can fall into cycles of conflict, failed communication, and a lack of emotional closeness within the marriage. Learn to love and appreciate **everything** about yourself and your spouse, for God intended them to be **just the way they are.**

> "Beloved, if God so loved us, we also ought to love one another. No one has ever seen God; if we love one another, God abides in us and His love is perfected in us."
> —1 John 4:11–12

The more we can grow in understanding about who we are mentally, emotionally, and spiritually, the less stress, anger, anxiety, and spiritual struggles we will experience in life. And the more you can intricately and intimately understand your spouse, the better and deeper your love for one another will be within your marital relationship. If you are interested, you can take your personalized temperament assessment by going to my website: www.thedivinemarriagebook.com. There is a cost for this analysis, as it is a formal and copyrighted assessment by Drs. Richard and Phyllis Arno. It will offer a specific explanation of your temperament in three different areas of life: social inclusion, control, and affection, along with brief personal recommendations based on your specific results; it is absolutely worth the investment!

Please also reference the appendix of this book to review helpful "Common Marriage Myths" to help give you a biblical mindset and a Godly lens in which to view your marriage.

Review

- Understanding your role as a husband or a wife will help you have less stress in your life and a better marriage.
- Understanding the strengths and weaknesses of your temperament will help you with self-forgiveness. You will grow in your spirituality, and you will learn to submit your weaknesses to God, allowing you to have less anxiety and more peace in your life.
- Understanding your spouse's temperament will help you relate to him/her, meet his/her needs more effectively, and have more tolerance for his/her shortcomings.
- God created you specifically: a role, a purpose, male or female, specific temperament, specific family of origin—nothing about you is a mistake!

✳ ✳ ✳

Heavenly Father,
I pray that as a couple we can gain insight and spiritual wisdom that will reveal love, appreciation, and forgiveness for one another; that this will restore past hurts and wounds to a state of healing and reconciliation within our marriage; and that love and appreciation for who You created us to be as a couple and as individuals will produce a stronger, deeper, and more loving relationship with one

another.
In Jesus's name we pray,
Amen.

2

A Knight in Shining Armor

"Deep in the heart, every man longs for a battle to fight, an adventure to live, and a beauty to rescue."
—John Eldredge, *Wild at Heart*

Every woman, whether she will admit it or not, wants a man to be her knight in shining armor. God made men to be the hero, and God made women to desire to be rescued. For generations, men have striven to be this knight in shining armor, and for decades upon decades women have been "wooed in the beginning" but eventually are left feeling disappointed and unloved further into the relationship. This idea of knighthood is a tall order for most men to live up to, and frankly the standards or expectations for men in the romantic relationship have become more and more difficult for them to attain in our modern society. Men are sent the message: "Be strong, be courageous, and make your family feel secure, but also be sensitive, loving, nurturing, and more intuitive."

This chapter is going to identify the **instinctual nature** of men and how it often "falls short" of the emotional, physical, and spiritual needs and expectations of a wife. These shortcomings thereby cause wives to request that men change their behavior, improve their approach, and increase their efforts so as to make wives feel

loved and **cherished**. God gave women the desire to feel like the number one priority in their husbands' eyes, and a woman feels this importance when she knows and believes her spouse loves her and prizes her above all else (besides God, of course) through his actions and his words.

> "Love isn't a state of perfect caring. It is an active noun like struggle. To love someone is to strive to accept that person exactly the way he or she is, right here and now."
> —Fred Rogers (from *Mr. Rogers' Neighborhood*)

Because it is in our basic human nature to return to our instinct and what is natural, men might be able to accommodate their wives' requests for a time, but then they will return to their nature of instinctual actions. For example, a wife may ask her husband to take her on a date once in awhile to help her feel special to him and help give them time to intimately and emotionally connect. He takes her on a wonderful date, and she enjoys it and feels more connected to her husband. Now she has the hope their relationship will improve with this new plan of having date nights more frequently.

But then life gets busy; there are family events and work obligations, and a month goes by with no date. The husband has now **failed** in the eyes of his wife and in his own. Then you have children, you start working opposite shifts to help compensate for daycare . . . the warfare on your quality time as a couple can become a serious problem. When this happens, a woman may start to feel that her husband does not care about her and she may become frustrated. A husband, who does not require the date night to be "ok" in the relationship, will look at this situation and have a logical answer like: "We are just too busy right now. We will get back on track . . . someday." This date is far more critical in the mind of a wife and will cause a desperation and resentment in her. Trying to cope with her feelings of rejection and disconnect from her husband, a wife might be saying to her mother, girlfriends, or a therapist: "What is wrong with my husband? I've told him a hundred times what I need. How can he not understand? Or is it that he does not care about me at all? How can he not see how important this is to our marriage?"

The Dumb-Guy Syndrome

I have heard from many men in marriage counseling, as well as **my own husband**, that trying to meet the needs of their wives can feel impossible and hopeless. Most men are not fashioned to understand and facilitate the emotional and intuitive needs of women. Even if we tell a man what we need or give him very strong hints, his brain and inner wirings are not like ours as women. Men can quickly forget or become confused, or it might not register with them at all how to emotionally care for their wife. Men are not naturally aware of the words, actions, or emotions they need to use to love and satisfy their wives. Now that mighty knight who made a woman fall in love with him has fallen from his place upon his steed into what frustrated wives everywhere would call the "dumb-guy" syndrome. Even though a wife can tell her husband over and over how he can make her feel loved or how he can be emotionally caring to her, he will forget, hurt her, or make her feel ignored and unimportant at some point in their relationship.

As a woman, being emotionally caring is natural. Women cannot comprehend how someone who says they love us could treat us so poorly by not "naturally" offering emotional care. A wife will begin to think a husband is doing this consciously or purposely unless she has the insight and wisdom about how men and women give and receive affection differently. Sometimes, even with this knowledge, **women will forget** the tendency of their husbands, as their desperation for affection and connection with their spouse will override their previously learned wisdom. It is equally crucial for a woman to forgive and understand her husband's efforts as it is for a husband to desire to achieve the goal of being her hero and loving his wife in all the ways she needs in order to feel safe and secure in the relationship.

The explanation of "dumb-guy syndrome" is meant to offer a bit of humor and insight for both men and women to this very frustrating situation: men are not as emotionally intuitive as women, and therefore men will often leave their wives feeling uncared for or unattended emotionally. Most husbands are not broken or purposefully ill-intentioned toward their wives. But men can also become frustrated and discouraged by not being able to please or satisfy their wives day after day, leading them to either give up or express their hopelessness in ways that would cause conflict or perhaps inflict more hurts and wounds with their harsh words or dismissive actions towards their wives.

Hopefully, the concept of a man's lack of relationship skills being instinctual rather than intentional allows wives to have more forgiveness and tolerance for the common and repeated ways men fail to meet their emotional needs; men are simply not wired to be relationship savvy or experts on female emotions. Often I will hear women say they want to give up asking or telling their husband what they need, because he just "doesn't get it" and it is too painful to keep asking and still not feel their husbands' care for them. Most women would even say this hurts more; to be vulnerable, ask, and then still not receive the emotional care is just too painful, so they simply stop asking. It is important for wives to consider how God designed our husbands and see him through the eyes of Christ: not failing them as women, but simply different than women and in need of wives' respect, understanding, and encouragement. Women are designed to be the relationship expert, and therefore we can never give up on trying to teach, inspire, and coach our spouse and children in this area of life. God has given wives a gift, and we are called to use it well.

For most women, taking care of others comes naturally, and because most people lack wisdom about how differently men and women are created, we begin to believe the other sex intentionally failed to meet our needs. A woman often believes her husband, whom she has been married to for many years, should just **know** what she needs. She knows how easily she can recognize the needs of others (husbands, children, the elderly, coworkers) every day, so how can he not do the same for her? When he does not do or say what she needs, even after she tries to remind him or respectfully request more attention, and then he continues to fail or fall short of her expectations, she will begin to believe it must be because he does not love her or care about her and that he is doing it intentionally. In an attempt to educate women about these instinctual and hardwired differences of how men and women give and receive love, the phrase "dumb-guy syndrome" fell out of my mouth and has been making women laugh in lighthearted agreement for years.

Woman-to-woman, we instantly understand what that means without an explanation of the phrase: men do not intend to hurt us or be neglectful, but they lack emotional intuitiveness and God did not make them as "relationship savvy" as women. Husbands, you are **not** dumb or stupid, but in times of conflict and miscommunication in your marriage, it will surely seem so to your wives.

A Line in the Sand

Husbands, if you are going to act out of instinct, you will most likely be naturally good at:

1. Working and pursuing a career
2. Feeling good when you earn a day's wage
3. Accomplishing tasks and goals
4. Being a problem-solver
5. Completing your life checklist: pursue and "acquire" a wife, a family, property, a career, and a nice vehicle
6. Protecting loved ones from harm
7. Feeling like a success and that your loved ones respect you; this is when you are "at your best."

Men get a sense of their identity and self-worth from their work, accomplishing tasks, and providing for their family. Men are designed to go to "war" to protect their family and feel a huge responsibility for their safety. Men are the leader: they are strong, courageous, and the "rock" of the family. They make authoritative decisions and have a strong sense of right and wrong, justice, and being logical. Because of this, men operate logically in daily life and in personal relationships, often lacking emotional sensitivity, and they require a significant level of respect from family, friends, and coworkers.

Instinctually men do not need to be taught how to identify the need for respect from other men. Men will naturally want respect from other men and recognize when they themselves are being disrespectful to others. There is an invisible but recognizable line in the sand for men in the area of respect, and they know the exact moment they cross it and are disrespectful to someone and the exact moment another man disrespects them. Men have a very clear choice: continue the disrespect and thereby suffer the consequences (foul language or even a fist to the face) or stop and allow the other person to have dominance. This whole process is not something that young boys are pulled aside and taught by their fathers. It is **inborn** and a natural way of interaction with others, especially man-to-man.

When a man is disrespectful to another man, they will have a heated argument—sometimes even physical assault. The last instinctual reaction a man can have is to retreat. But retreating comes at a heavy spiritual and emotional price for men; when a man backs down after being disrespected, he will feel weak, worthless, and like a failure. The thoughts in his head do not make him feel very good about himself. When a husband is disrespected by his wife, he will react in the same way. Hopefully he is able to restrain himself from physical assault, but verbal harshness and hurtful words, sometimes swearing, can happen. It is **that** important for a man to be respected. It seems like an overstatement to wives. In fact, every wife could probably recall a time when her husband became extremely angry with her for something she said and she might think to herself, "I didn't think it was **that** offensive, or I didn't mean to upset him." Some very controlled and well-intentioned husbands do not want to lash out verbally at their wives, so they will choose to retreat. This means a husband will shut down and not talk, walk away, or even get in his car and leave to avoid any further conflict with his wife. It does not feel any better to a man to make the choice to retreat during conflict with his wife than it would a male peer. In fact, it is worse, because of how much he loves her. The thoughts in his head tell him he is weak, his wife shouldn't treat him this way, she walks all over him, he can't keep letting her do this to him, etc. The wife, on the other hand, feels like her husband abandoned her in her time of need, and he must not really care about her at all to just leave, walk away, or ignore her.

This male instinctual behavior and language related to respect are as foreign to us as women as our emotions and "crazy" behaviors are to men. We do not see the line in the sand and very often have no idea how or when we cross it by being disrespectful with our words or actions. But this skill can and **must** be learned in order to have a good and functional relationship with your husband.

"Wives, submit to your own husbands, as you do the Lord."
—Ephesians 5:22

God instructs us to be respectful and submissive, as it is not always natural for us. Scripture does **not** directly state, "Wives, love your husbands," because it is already in our nature to love. But God knew wives would need reminding to be submissive and respectful to our husbands. If we cannot, in the moment, find it within ourselves to do it out of love or respect for him, then we would do so because we want to please the Lord.

"Husbands, love your wives, as Christ loved the church and gave himself up for her."
—Ephesians 5:25

Being loving is not necessarily in the *nature of men*. So God knew he would have to order men to do so. Husbands, what would it look like to love your wives like Christ loved the church? Frankly, husbands, it means sacrifice and the dying of "self-concern." This also means acting out of wisdom, learning all about your wife and how to care for her and sacrificing your own needs and instincts to meet the needs of your wife. So many men have goodwill and good intentions toward their wives and the marriage but feel helpless or hopeless in trying to meet the needs of this "foreign being" called woman.

Kind and Gentle

One of the most helpful skills a wife can learn is how to be respectful to her husband. It is surprising to me how quickly a woman's emotions can override her intention to be respectful—me included—and therefore we need to recruit God's help in this endeavor. Not only do our daily life, parenting stress, finance distress, and marital needs cause us to verbally vomit on our husbands, but there are spiritual forces against us. Every day, women are under attack in our minds to uncontrollably launch disrespectful words at our husbands, with the intention to connect with and be understood by him. A woman's ultimate goal in conflict is to have emotional resolution and reinstate the emotional bond between herself and her husband; instead, the conversation ends in a screaming match, and the husband is so offended he leaves, or he is mean or hurtful with his words in return. Sound familiar?

I know that when I read a self-help book, I want practical suggestions. This is one subject where it might be helpful for women to understand specific ways to show respect to their husbands. One example suggested by Dr. Emerson Eggerichs (author of *Love and Respect*, a book I would highly recommend) is for a wife to write a letter to her husband, telling him all the things she respects about him. This idea is similar to the wooing love letters many of us long to get from our husbands, but since a man's love language is respect, the letter would compliment him in the ways you respect him. For our first wedding anniversary, I made Scott a plaque that was entitled, "101 Ways I Respect You," with both funny and sincere ways I respected him. There were phrases such as "I respect the decisions you make for our family" and "I respect you when you joyfully eat the leftovers in the fridge." He couldn't believe I thought of 101 things, and I am not sure if he ever read through them all completely, but he said it was the best gift he had ever received. Another way to show respect to your husband is to not point out when he makes mistakes—to be quiet and overlook his failures—and then be encouraging and affirming when he does things well.

In the area of parenting, a golden rule for wives is to differ with our husbands in private and not in front of our children. You are learning in this chapter how important it is for a man to be respected, especially by his wife and children, and to criticize or make him look foolish in front of your children is one of the greatest wounds a wife can inflict upon her husband. Trusting your husband to make good decisions on your behalf is a wonderful way to show him respect; that might be in the form of finances, making a move in living conditions or a new business venture, or even deciding to switch to a new church. Wives can certainly have an opinion, and their input in decisions in the marriage is very valuable, but the final decision should be the husbands', and everyone in the family should be honoring and supportive of that decision. I know this can be a difficult task at times, especially if you do not agree with the decisions your husband is making. But, with faith, a woman can have confidence that God will do the correcting of her husband, and she will be especially blessed for fulfilling a role that can be incredibly difficult. A wife has great power and influence with her children, and we often set the tone for how the family acts and reacts to our husbands. We have a great responsibility then to teach our children and extended family and friends to always talk about our husbands in a positive way. That means when you need to vent, the best place to bring those grievances is first to God and then your husband in a respectful way. No more "husband-bashing" on girls' weekends, with your mom on the phone, or to your Bible study gals. Now, if you are looking to a spiritual mentor or fellow Christian wife for advice, that is different than just complaining. We should be there for each other and encourage one another on this very difficult journey of being a submissive and respectful wife. One of my favorite writers in this area is Elizabeth George. I would recommend any of her books to have a deeper understanding of how to accept and thrive in the role of a respectful wife, which is the role God intended for us. There is so much more peace, rest, and security through settling into this role than trying to be **everything, to everyone, all the time**, which is what I believe is the message most women receive today.

> "Do not let your adorning be external—the braiding of hair and the putting on of gold jewelry, or the clothing you wear—but let your adorning be the hidden person of the heart with the imperishable beauty of a gentle and quiet spirit, which in God's sight is very precious."
> —1 Peter 3:3–4

Wives are called by God to be quiet, gentle, and respectful to their husbands. For many of us, that is easier said than done. Not that most women aren't kind, or that we don't have a gentleness about us that men cannot replicate, but daily life, especially in this day and age, causes women to have so many other worries, stressors, and emotions that don't exactly leave us looking like Mother Teresa. Some women would argue, "This quiet and timid creature just isn't me." The truth is, all women have to put effort into being more kind and respectful with our words. Just like I have asked your husbands to seek wisdom in learning about your emotional mind and have better communication with you, I would ask women to root it in their hearts to be kind and gentle with their words to their husband and their families, even when your emotions tell you to say or do otherwise.

"Pleasant words are a honeycomb sweetness to the soul and health to the body."
—*Proverbs 16:24*

As wives, we can all surely admit that we are not perfect, and there will be times when our stress and emotions get the best of us and we will inevitably be disrespectful to our husbands. Two things need to happen: apologize and ask for his forgiveness as soon as you see something you said upset him, and then ask God to help you watch your tongue and control your words in the future. We all need God's help to be the best wives we can be. There is a very important piece of doctrine to subscribe to in order to have the **desire** to be respectful: respect for your husband is **not** earned. Out in the world that might be the general rule, but between husband and wife that simply is not the case. God ordered men to love their wives like Christ loved the church. He did not say, "Love her only if she deserves it." As God ordered wives to respect their husbands, He did not say, respect him only if he earns it. Men love their wives and wives respect their husbands because it is pleasing to God and it is a way in which we can be Christ-like to one another. When women truly believe it is their calling to be respectful, their attitude, words, and nature will simply be more kind and gentle. And again, on days when it is difficult, this is a very good opportunity to call on God's supernatural power and ask the Holy Spirit that dwells within us to be our guide in overcoming our need for emotional validation or proving how "awful" our husband is treating us. Rather, we will be respectful and ask the Holy Spirit to gently remind our husbands of their faults rather than our disrespect or resentments towards them. I would also encourage women that it is much easier to watch their words and behaviors in order to not be disrespectful and cause conflict with your husband, than it is to try to forgive and let go of the hurtful things their husband might say to them in the midst of conflict after feeling disrespected.

I know when I first started to make a greater effort to watch my words to my husband, I was thinking of how I could talk to him in a way that I could still express my concerns, emotions, or needs and still meet his need to be respected.

Here are a few sentence structures I have found to be helpful in communicating respectfully with my husband:

1. I have been struggling with some of my emotions, can you just listen to how I feel and help me sort things out?

2. The thoughts in my head are making me feel mad or upset with you. I don't want to feel that way, but this is what I keep thinking about . . .

3. I have some unresolved feelings about our relationship, and I don't want them to cause problems or distance in our relationship. Can we talk about them?

4. I need your reassurance because I am feeling like you do not care about me and that I am not important to you. I know that you do not **try** to make me feel that way, but here are some examples of what would really help me feel better . . .

5. I could really use your reassurance and appreciation that I am a good wife/mother/ Christian/person today. I am feeling attacked in my mind/my emotions, and you always make me feel more grounded and that things in life will be ok.

6. You know what I really miss? When you used to (fill in the blank) that always makes me feel so loved, valued, and cher-

ished by you.

A great resource for women is *The Respect Dare* by Nina Roesner, which includes daily challenges in how to be respectful to your husband. It was written in a similar style to *The Love Dare* by Alex and Stephen Kendrick. *The Love Dare* is also a wonderful resource and was produced as a companion to their movie *Fireproof* (an excellent movie about the struggles in marriage) in 2008.

I mentioned only a few ways to become more respectful as a wife, but even more effective advice than to make a list of respectful and disrespectful words or actions is for wives to prepare their hearts and minds each day to be respectful by asking for God's guidance and protection in this pursuit. My personal prayer is listed below, and I believe it has helped me immensely to become a kind and respectful wife. When I go too long without praying about it, I find myself in the midst of heated conflict with my spouse. I have learned to criticize less, resist my temptation to say something I will regret, and withhold releasing my stress onto my husband and have learned to deal with my emotions on my own and with God, then present my concerns to my husband in a calm and respectful manner. This can be scary for women, and it might feel like our husband "deserves" to know how he made us feel, but this is a precious piece of wisdom and an expensive lesson to learn for most marriages; this kind of heated emotion will not end well, and a woman rarely receives the validation she is looking for from her spouse when he feels he is being attacked by her emotionally. It is always prudent to look to God's Word for direction. As the following verse states, we can win our husbands over with our respectful and kind attitudes more than our nagging or negative words. Even if your husband is not obeying God, Scripture says he can still be won over and changed by the power of a respectful wife!

"Likewise, wives, be subject to your own husbands, so that even if some do not obey the word, they may be won without a word by the conduct of their wives, when they see your respectful and pure conduct."
—1 Peter 3: 1–2

Review

- Every woman desires to be cherished and a priority in the eyes of her husband.
- Wives need to understand men are not relationship savvy and have grace and forgiveness for our husbands when they fall short of their expectations or do not meet their emotional needs in the way we would prefer.
- Women can become skilled at being respectful, but men need to understand women do not see the "line in the sand."
- A Godly woman will desire to be kind and gentle with her words as a powerful influence in the family and especially within the marital relationship.

* * *

Prayer for Wives

Dear Father in Heaven,
Help me to be the submissive and respectful wife You desire me to be. I am submitted and obedient to You, Father God, and believe it is my calling to live out this role to please you and my husband. There are times when I am scared and feel I need my husband to know how he hurts me, so he will not keep doing it. In these times, please use the Holy Spirit to convict my husband to come to me and be loving and caring to me. Loose upon me in those

same times Your love, assurance, comfort, and courage that I will always have the love, approval, and affection I need when I come to You first. Lord Jesus, in times of emotional stress in my marriage, I ask you to have one arm around my shoulder and a hand over my mouth. Do not allow the Enemy to trick or deceive me into being disrespectful to my husband. Help me to be less focused on my feelings and the needs I "think" will make me happy, and rather, focus on what You desire for my life. Redirect me to focus on You and Your power within my marriage. Teach me to be like You, Jesus, selfless and forgiving in every way. Continue to refine me, Lord, to the kind, pure and respectful wife you intended me to be. I believe I can do it with Your help and the strength of Christ within me.

I pray this in Jesus's name.

Amen.

3

Do You Really Love Me?

"'Do you really love me?' means, 'Will you accept me in process? Will you embrace what is different about me and applaud my efforts to become? Can I just be human— strong and vibrant some days, weak and frail on others? [. . .] Will you love me even when I disappoint you?'"
—Angela Thomas, *Do You Think I'm Beautiful? The Question Every Woman Asks*

I believe most women just want to know and believe their husbands care about them. A wife's innermost desire (planted within them by God) is to be cherished and treasured above all else. It is the same pursued feeling we have when men court us in order to become married. Most men we counsel will reply with something like, "Well, that seems like a lot of work. I need to pursue my wife everyday?" It can be a daunting task for a husband to pursue his wife for the rest of his life in a marriage. Some men, based on their temperament, are naturally better at pursing or being romantic than others, but it is an essential skill for men to acquire and a necessary component of a successful marriage for every man to master.

The biblical counsel in this area is this:

1. You are called, by God, to "give up your life for your wife" like

Christ gave His life for you. (Ephesians 5:25)

2. There is more joy in serving others than getting your own "self-ish" needs met. (Acts 20:35)

3. Once both the husband and the wife have wisdom about the strengths and weaknesses of each of the sexes, as well as im-proved/open communication, meeting each other's needs is easier and more fulfilling than you could ever have imagined. (Phil 2:3–4) This chapter will offer some concrete and practical ways a husband can **prove** to his wife that he really loves her.

I have used the following subchapters to help men understand the many ways a woman will feel loved by her husband. (You might notice there is some kind of musical song title theme to these categories. Another female intricacy: we love to relate music and dancing to **everything** in life. I didn't even realize it until I was finished writing the chapter.)

My Favorite Things

A man asks his girlfriend when they are dating what some of her favorite things are. She tells him her favorite flowers, her favorite color, the scent of candles she likes or her favorite restaurant. The pursuing man listens intently as she hints and reacts with approval when he later surprises her with one of these gestures and he "gets it right." He does an excellent job of showing her attention and making her feel like she is the most important thing in his world by giving her gifts or planning dates to include her favorite things while courting her. Unfortunately, often just a few years into the marriage, the wife cannot remember the last time she received flowers, her husband complains when she buys candles because they "stink up the house and are a waste of money," and the only restaurants they go to are ones with big screen TVs hanging from the walls. He does not notice her new outfit, and they do not even talk to each other as they eat.

Husbands, we wives desperately need to be "wooed" for the rest of our lives! Husbands can cause a lot of hurt in a wife and feelings of unworthiness in their wife by a husband not remembering these valuable things about her. The alternative is you can be a total stud and make her swoon for you all over again when you meet her needs, by remembering some of her "favorites things." Small gestures like this can make a huge difference in the closeness of your relationship. These acts of love also offer protection from hidden, internal resentments within your wife that tend to build up over the years and cause bitterness and distance in the marriage. For example, your wife will begin to notice how kind you are to the neighbor lady shoveling her walkway, or when you give a compliment to the waitress, or when you remember who won Super Bowl III, but you just happen to forget what perfume she wears.

Gifts do not need to be constant or expensive, but paying attention to her when she talks about things/activities she likes—and then surprising her with them every once in awhile—will earn you a bajillion bonus points in her book. Remember—your wife wants you to intimately know her, better than anyone else knows her; this is how she will feel most connected to you. Planning a date at least once a month is extremely important. For you, the husband, planning the date means you decide where you are going (based on what she likes and what you believe would be most pleasing to her) and **you** arrange the babysitter. Taking her to a romantic or new restaurant and perhaps dancing or a live band or a walk through a park will fulfill her need to be alone with you and will also give the relationship the sense of passion and adventure that every woman desires. There are amazing dating and gift idea websites, so take advantage of them. A note on the bathroom mirror, a gas station rose, or a candy bar—it all counts in our emotional inventory of whether we believe our husband takes time out of his busy day to think of us and make us feel like we are a priority to him.

Let's Get Physical

Hold on, it's not what you think, gentlemen . . . Most women like physical affection as a sign of affirmation and feeling loved, but in "girl language" that means hugs, holding hands, foot or shoulder massages, and cuddling on the couch. Dumb-guy move number 329: because your wife desires and accepts physical affection from you, it must be a secret signal she wants to have sex. Sometimes any hint of physical affection seems like a good sign or encouragement by your wife in getting **your** physical needs met too, but hold off on that idea for now and we will better address this issue in the sex chapter. Oh yes, there is a chapter on sex. For now, just take my word for it, it is worth your time and restraint to show physical affection to your wife without sexual advances to help meet her needs for physical affection and to help her feel cared for by you so that she **actually desires** to have sex with you ever again.

I think most women I counsel would agree that a good, strong hug from our spouse is one of the best feelings ever. It satisfies so many areas of a wife's needs: we feel his strength, we feel safe, we feel assured that he is there for us and that no matter what he will protect us, and we can trust that it will all turn out ok. Husbands—did you know a hug could do all that? Foot and shoulder massages help us to relax and also show us you want to serve us; we often feel, as women, that we are always serving everyone else with little attention paid to our needs. Handholding is something you can do in church, in the car, and out in public that symbolizes that we **belong** to you, you want to be close to us, and that you are really "in it" (life) with us. If you really want to blow our socks off, a good, passionate kiss once and awhile will do a marriage good. Daily hello and goodbye kisses will help to keep romance alive and "prime" the passion engine for later. It is important to discuss with your wife how much physical attention she needs. Some women need more physical affection than others, and many women are very particular in how they like to receive their physical affection. Test these areas with your wife and ask her what she needs **today** to get her physical needs for affection met. Try not to view this as high maintenance, but as just another way a wife desires her husband to pursue her, communicate with her, and intricately know her on a deep and personal level.

The Wall

Most women are pretty good at expressing their feelings and emotional needs, but it is important to know that there are temperament types in which the woman will rarely express her desires or feelings verbally. She will want her husband to read her mind, which leaves her feeling bitter and resentful that her spouse doesn't care about her when he does not deliver the emotional care she desires. A husband might have no idea he is failing his wife if she is not expressing it. If a wife tries to express her needs to her husband and he does not offer understanding or validation or show behaviors that are reassuring to his wife and her emotional state, over time she will give up trying to connect with him. This is called "putting up a wall."

Husbands, your wife is emotionally based and she can only endure so much emotional hurt before she starts to protect herself from the pain of rejection or neglect. Your wife was NOT created to be a warrior and her constant connection with her feelings and emotions leaves her vulnerable and quite easily wounded.

A woman might build an emotional barrier based on her feelings of hopelessness that you will never truly understand her or meet her emotional needs. She might do this because she has been verbally discouraged from asking you to meet her needs, or it might be her **perception** based on feeling rejection or neglect in meeting her emotional needs. Many women might put up a wall after conflict, especially heated and hurtful conflict in which her husband might have been harsh or even verbally abusive towards her. It might be coming from her childhood or past relationships in which she was ignored, neglected, or rejected by men, and now this wound is being transferred and compounded by events and interactions that are similar in the marriage.

There are many reasons a woman begins to build a wall. As her husband, you should be aware of this, concerned for her, and pursuing her to prevent it from becoming permanent. This "wall" is a dangerous place for a woman to be, because once she starts protecting herself from the pain, it usually means there are hidden resentments towards her husband. Distance will begin to grow between them. This process is usually very slow and unnoticeable at first; layer by layer, one brick at a time, the divider will go up. The biggest factors in women feeling the need to protect themselves are a lack of emotional resolution in conflict and repeated emotional pain within the marital relationship. Emotional resolution after conflict (no matter how large or small) and ensuring sure the wife feels understood by her husband **are the most important** components to securing a strong and positive emotional bond in the marriage, which is what allows your wife to feel loved and secure in the relationship. Over time, both men and women can become discouraged if they continue to fail to find resolution to conflict. This will lead the husband to try to ignore or avoid conflict, and the unresolved issues will cause the wife to shut down and stop trying to get her emotional needs met, leaving the couple disconnected and distant.

Sometimes a man will see the lack of his wife's demand to interact or connect as a reprieve from conflict. He may even **enjoy** the "break" from her requests or the arguments these demands typically cause. A man might think, "This is great! She isn't screaming at me or needing anything from me. This is the happiest we have been in years." Beware, men. This often means your wife is pulling away and giving up on the emotional connection and perhaps even giving up on the marriage.

The **wisdom** women need to remember is that your husbands are **not**, I repeat, **not** naturally honed in on emotionally needs, but wives are. Many women argue this is unfair, but God made women to be more relationship intuitive than men. Although the husband should be the spiritual leader and pursuer in the relationship, when it comes to making sure the relationship is "tidy" (clean of any conflict, anger, bitterness, or grief that might be lurking in the corners), women should take on the role of pursuing resolution to conflict and making sure their husbands understand how they feel. (I know, ladies—just another thing we need to keep clean!) Wives, this is for your own protection. Women do not do well with leftover internalized feelings. In the moment they might say to themselves, "Oh, I'll just get over it and suck it up," but later, wives can experience bitterness, unforgiveness, and a lack of affection for their husbands, and it always comes from unresolved feelings. It is always easier to prevent the wall from going up than to try to take it down later. In my experience of fifteen years of marriage counseling, it is the number one reason women will seek a divorce; they can no longer see hope in removing the many layers of protection they have put between themselves and their husband after repeated hurts and many unresolved emotions.

Women can struggle with the idea of the role of being responsible for emotional resolution, and it can make them feel like they have to **beg** or **force** their husband to meet their emotional needs. "Do I really need to do that?" they will ask me in counseling. Wives, no matter how often we tell our husbands what we need or how we need to feel loved by them, they will eventually fall into their instinctually nature or behavior patterns and fail us. (Just as we will become overly emotional at times and fail **them** by being disrespectful.) This should be a reminder to us, as wives, of two things:

1. We need to rely on God to meet our needs when our husbands do not.

2. Because we are naturally more emotional and relationship savvy, we need to be responsible for getting our needs met and we **cannot** give up on trying to communicate these needs to our husband in **respectful ways** that they can understand, even if it is uncomfortable or difficult to verbalize.

Husbands, if your wife has stopped seeking affection or an emotional connection with you, **call your local crisis marriage counseling team immediately!** Okay, maybe you do not have to panic right away, but understand you need to pursue your wife emotionally. God designed you to do it, be the leader, and be responsible for her. You did it well at one point, or she would have never married you in the first place.

Husbands, try to remember the ways your wife has told you how she feels or what things are upsetting to her, or just ask her again. We love it when our husbands pursue us by asking and trying to understand how we feel! Women can go from contemplating divorce to completely falling in love with her husband again simply by feeling heard, **understood,** and pursued **relentlessly** by their spouse. (True story, I have seen it happen within our marriage counseling couples, time and time again.) This can be a difficult task to ask of a husband, especially if it seems like she is not responding or she is full-on rejecting him. But be resilient: "And let us not grow weary of doing good, for in due season we will read, if we do not give up," (Galatians 6:9).

That whole emotional wall can come falling down in a glorious crash in an instant, and the emotional bond between husband and wife can be restored! Both men and women need to be encouraged by this, because sometimes as a wife you feel like you could never feel the same way about your husband because of the emotional pain and the layers of hurts and wounds that have built up over many months or years. And for husbands, it starts to feel hopeless and you might feel like your wife will never come back to you, but God's formula for the connection between husband and wife will never fail! Hope comes to us through wisdom, by understanding the nature of one another and then applying these ideas and skills. Choose to forgive one another, and by the grace of God, it will lead you to a better-than-you-ever-thought-possible kind of marriage!

I Need A Hero

Deep down, every woman needs her husband to be her hero! And, if men are truly honest with themselves, they kind of enjoy feeling like one too! As cheesy and fairytale-romance as it sounds, God intended for women to be pursued, taken care of, and "rescued" by a man. In today's society, women and young girls are given the message that we don't really need a man and we can do it all by ourselves. Women today work full-time, take care of the home, do the laundry, cook, clean, and take kids to their events, sports, and music lessons. On top of all that, most wives try to be involved in the community and their church and attend a scrapbooking or cake-decorating class "just for fun." Sheesh. (Where are our super-hero capes?) So when all that is said and done, she needs her man to rescue her from a life of hectic busyness and chaos by doing a few simple things:

1. Take on the burden of financial responsibility for the family. Either manage all the finances or ensure your wife has your support emotionally and financially so as to not have her be stressed with or have the fear of not having enough money. Men are the more strategic and logical thinkers in the marital unit, and you have great influence in bringing reassurance, sanity, and security to an already emotionally frazzled wife. Expressing your concern for money or putting pressure on your wife to resolve money issues is not helpful. Rather, try to insulate and protect her from this additional stressor. This is an area of strength for most men, and, if it is not one of your strengths, pursue it and become responsible for the financial security of your family.

2. Women need their husbands to be the disciplinarian with their children. Nothing feels worse than having to be "the heavy" as a mom. Wives were created by God to love and nurture children, not to be harsh with them. Every woman I counsel that has children will at some point comment (out of frustration), "Why do kids always listen better to their father than me?" The main answer is because God made men to be the head of the household, and they have a spiritual authority with their child that is unspoken. It is important to consider and understand how difficult it is for some women to allow their husbands to be the one to discipline. One reason for this is, to us as mothers, the husband will seem overly harsh or mean to the children. Because of how much we love and instinctually protect our children, we can become critical of how our hus-

bands choose to discipline the children. It is valuable for men to have a framework of being authoritative with their children, but also love them as God loves them, even when they need discipline. Some men are truly too harsh and even borderline abusive with their children due to a lack of a healthy parenting style in their own childhood or due to stress or other issues. Parenting education is helpful for both husbands and wives to ensure you are both on the same page and offering your child the best parenting possible.

I highly recommend two valuable parenting resources: *Total Transformation* by Dr. James Lehman and *Spiritual Parenting* by Michelle Anthony. Both of these parenting resources will empower you as a couple and guide you in parenting your children effectively, despite your past parenting issues or your own experiences as a child. Being unified as a parental unit is crucial to having a successful marriage and in achieving a well-behaved child. Many churches offer seminars or small groups for parents and stepparents.

Sometimes it is necessary for a wife to discipline if her husband is not home. Some tricks for women to try are: Have a low, more monotone voice when disciplining children (they will respond better than to a more fluctuating tone, as children are instinctual too and if they detect emotion, they will try to use it against you.) The stern, more robotic facial expressions are very effective on children, as it leaves little room for manipulation. Please realize wives struggle in this area because God designed them to be **emotional**, and trying to control the expression on your face and the tone in your voice is like asking a man to never scratch himself! In other words, it is practically impossible. Part of the wisdom and counsel in this book is to help men and women realize their roles, and when they fall in line with them, life is much easier and takes less effort. It is not in a mother's "nature" to be void of emotion and treat others harshly, so a wife alone with children all day or after a child's tantrum can be extremely stressful, and she needs the comfort and encouragement of her husband. It is important for all of us to accept how God made us, and for us not to feel like a failure or ineffective as a husband or a wife. Parenting can be a huge stressor on a marriage and the best approach is to have good education in specific parenting skills, social support in order to be able to have breaks, and to always be supportive and encouraging to one another, completely unified as parents.

Just the Way You Are

So how many comedians have an "act" that makes fun of the dumb things men say to their wives? Or how many sitcoms poke fun of a husband's remarks that were unintentionally insensitive to their wives? Making hurtful comments about a wife's looks or weight or comparing the wife to another woman are deadly mistakes made by men everywhere. We all know these are common errors that men make, and that is why they can be humorous. And yet, this issue is no joke. I often hear in counseling, that couples have conflict about what a husband has said to his wife "ever-so-innocently," that made her feel not good enough or unlovable. Understand this, husbands: evil, negative thoughts have set up camp in the head of every woman around a feeling of not being good enough, thin enough, pretty enough—the list goes on and on. Even women with good self-confidence who are well rooted in Christ can be left feeling less than desirable or valued by their husband due to minor, innocent comments he might make to her.

Trying to explain this to husbands can make them feel paranoid; perhaps, they think, they shouldn't say anything or that they shouldn't even try to give their wife a compliment. My husband would call this "walking on eggshells" for husbands. More than once in our own learning curve of our marriage, he would say, "I didn't know saying something like **that** would make you upset." I think giving an example at this point would be helpful; I am a pretty average-sized woman, not overweight and not super thin, but pretty confident that I am attractive to my husband. But, like most men, my husband can forget to give me compliments or give me verbal affirmations about by physical appearance . . . that is, until I start dieting or exercising more often. Then, all of a sudden, he is Mr. Compliments Galore. In his defense, he would say, "I am just trying to be supportive." Ok guys, here comes the "women are crazy" part. In **my head**, all I am hearing is, "Sure, I wasn't good enough or thin enough before to remind him to give me a compliment, but now that I am dieting and working out he notices me? He was probably totally disgusted by me before and that is why he never said anything nice. He is probably complimenting me a lot now because he doesn't want me to stop losing weight and he just wants me to look perfect all the time!" Husbands, the thoughts go on and on in our heads like this. **You have no idea.**

A female's thoughts and feelings work in this way: our deep, heart and soul's desire is to be loved, cherished, and prized about all else by our husbands . . . **just the way we are.** We need to feel loved for all our quirky behaviors, all of our difficult character flaws and emotional weaknesses, and, most of all, for how we look. A husband that can make his wife "feel" beautiful will have a wife that will strive to look and feel beautiful herself, and then she will do it in healthy ways and not self-defeating ones. A woman that was not loved or accepted by her father, or who was hurt by another man at a young age, will often carry this wound into the marriage; along with it, mostly likely, will be unhealthy eating patterns or poor self-image problems. A woman needs to have healing from Jesus first, to know and believe she is precious and beautiful in His eyes, but then she also needs this affirmation from her husband. I have seen many, many women learn to love themselves and look and feel better than they ever have by acquiring these two areas of love and approval: their Heavenly Father first, and their husband second. Many women cannot lose weight because of their self-hatred or feelings of rejection, and a husband has great power and influence in how he makes his wife feel about herself. (Dads, this is equally important for you to do for your daughters.)

Most men cannot understand how wives can become so emotional over something that they would consider as being so minor or unimportant. Here is an example: After a wife has had a tough day at work or at home with the kids all day, her husband comes home from work, and he is greeted with a grimace and instant complaints from his wife. While a "Welcome home, honey" and a peck on the cheek would be preferred by her husband, due to a wife's need for affirmation and comfort from her husband, she is ready to launch the erupting volcano all over her poor, unsuspecting spouse the moment he walks through the door. Out of his own frustration, a husband might be tempted to say, "What is your problem, woman? You are **always** so crabby and negative. I just want to come home and not feel stressed out by you." Our inner hope as a wife is that our husband will love us unconditionally, and being told we are "always" something (negative, crabby, angry, sad, etc.) and a burden to our husband makes us feel rejected and not good enough as his wife.

The solution is to make your wife feel like she is strong, important, and a valued daughter of the King in moments of her emotional trials and natural weaknesses. The ability for a husband to lift his wife up in her weak moments (but not identify her as being weak) can help define the emotional bond between them and improve the overall strength of their marriage. This is also good advice for strengthening and enhancing your wife's self-confidence. **This is an important tip**: the weight of your words and actions are mighty; one crucial moment could equal days/years of hurt and pain for a wife if she feels rejected, or it could mean a lifetime of a fulfilling and satisfying marriage if done well. Take notes, gentlemen!

What does it **truly** mean to love your wife **just the way she is?** Well, it means you should not try to understand her through your male-logical brain, but rather try to see her through God's perspective. He made her wondrous and beautiful just the way she is, and if you can try to see that her **weaknesses** are placed in her by God's design and see them as strengths as well, then you will begin to see your wife through a whole new lens. When your wife is "crabby," say to yourself, "She is in need of emotional comfort." God made women emotionally based to enable them to care and nurture children, nurse the sick and elderly, and offer comfort to the many in need in this world. Due to her emotional composition, a wife typically does not endure a lot of stress well, but you, as her unfailing superhero-husband (da da dun dun da da) can help relieve her stress and anxiety with words of comfort, affirmation, and a good, strong hug. What a different and refreshing scenario than a man's instincts would provide: the husband comes home, sees his wife is crabby, avoids her, and after she sighs and slams enough cabinet doors he asks, "What's wrong with you?" (Umm . . . husbands, that's always bad. Don't ever say, "What's your problem?", "What's your deal?", or "What is wrong with you?") The wife then "blasts" her husband with all her day's stress and emotions, which feels attacking and disrespectful to him, and World War III begins. This scenario proves to the husband that it is better to just not ask and proves to the wife her husband just doesn't care about her and doesn't try to understand her. Maybe she thinks, "We should just give up all together in trying to connect with each other." (Reference back to "The Wall").

Everything I Do, I Do it For You

Husbands, this should be your daily battle cry. With biblical wisdom, a resigned heart, and a submitted will to be pleasing to God, it must be your **intention** to take on the role of **emotional caretaker** for your wife. God's Word calls men to, "Love your wives, as Christ loved the church," (Ephesians 5:25) and what did Jesus do for us? He gave up His life for us. Husbands are called to do many difficult tasks, submit themselves to sacrifice for their wives, and act selflessly "out of reverence for Christ." (Ephesians 5:21)

What does it mean to be the "caretaker" of your wife's emotional well-being? Well, it means that you do not try to be her "boss" and tell her what to do to fix the problem, you do not try to be her "counselor" and give her a lecture on how she should just "not feel that way," and you do not act as her "condemner" and make her feel like she is wrong, bad, or weak for feeling the way she feels. A wife needs her husband to take on the role of comforter and encourager of her overall emotional well-being. A Godly husband wants to take on this role and not allow others to meet his wife's needs in this way: not her mother, not her girlfriends, and hopefully not that "way-too-nice-guy" at her workplace. Women emotionally care for the rest of the world all day long. At least that is how it can feel when her needs are not being cared for properly. A "well-loved" wife will feel full of energy and have the ability to serve others, because that is what God created her to do, and it is wonderful for her to actually feel fulfilled by doing it! But an emotionally neglected wife will feel taken advantage of, unappreciated, and that people are draining her, requiring her to serve others without the emotional "steam" to do it. A wife that can trust her husband to care for her emotions and rely on him to build her up in times of trouble is literally unstoppable!

First, it is so important to understand how your wife was designed by God and what her purpose is in God's kingdom and not apply **your own understanding**.

> "Trust in the Lord with all your heart, and do not lean on your own understanding."
> —Proverbs 3:5

As we just referenced in the last section, try to remember that God created women to be emotional, because they will love and nurture your children better with an "emotional" approach than your logical "harshness." Women are also the caregivers in this world and without that emotional component there would be no one to make others feel cared for and we, as a world, would lack compassion, empathy, and relational cohesiveness. I will repeat that often in this book, because if you can consistently remind yourself of that, you can apply the "logic" of this idea in times when it would be easy to feel offended, disrespected or emotional as men, during conflict with your wife. Just as a woman needs to respect you for your leadership, strength, and logical thinking, so must men accept she was created by God to be emotional, passionate, and intense. I use the word "intense" because it is a positive way of describing how a man sees a woman when she is reacting in full-force with her emotions. It is irrational and unhelpful in the eyes of a man, but it is undeniable how a woman's natural wiring, how tired she is, the events of the day, or the time of the month might effect her emotional reaction. When a woman sees emotions like this in others, it usually does not bother her and she seems to know exactly how to soothe and comfort the other person. But to men, it can seem like trying to tame a wild animal.

Husbands, there will come a time when you marvel at her ability to love, care for, and empathize with others. Then there will be times when you struggle with her irrational thoughts and extreme feelings, and you will feel helpless in your ability to soothe her. The first step is that you accept with your heart, mind, and soul that this is who God created your wife to be and she is not a mistake. She does not need to be fixed. You as her husband have great influence in being able to build her up and help her flourish, or you can reject this perspective, make her feel crazy and not good enough, and struggle with conflict throughout your marriage.

So are you ready for a "golden nugget" of advice? Wisdom-seeking men, it is easy as this: Listen to your wife when she talks, and try not to solve or judge in your head. Only listen to her words, and try to understand how she feels by watching her mood and emotions as she talks. You could start out saying something like, "So what I heard you say was . . . ," "It sounds like you are really upset about . . . ," or "I am so proud of you for dealing with . . ." Just these phrases alone will make your wife feel important and valued by you. Then, tell her you **heard** what she said, even repeating parts of her conversation back to her (because then we really believe you were **actually** listening), then affirm her by saying she is good, strong, or incredible for going through what she is going through emotionally and that you cannot imagine what that must be like for her (because you cannot, as you are logical and not as emotional), and then reassure her and **pray for her** that everything will work out and be ok, because she has you and God on her side!

Most men would admit at times it is difficult to pay attention to or "track" their wives because of how their minds seem to jump topics or give too many details. This is where the **skilled** husband shines. He can "hang in there" while his wife vents or tells her story, and then he can simply paraphrase, affirm, or encourage her when she is done and then look for signs that she is emotionally satisfied. A comical example of this: My husband and I were on vacation a couple of years ago, lying on a beach in Fort Lauderdale. I was telling my husband about some deep, spiritual realization I had come to the night before while spending time in prayer with God. Without hesitation, he says, "Honey, do you see that? It's the Goodyear Blimp. I wonder if it is hard to fly one of those things . . ." Because my husband is a pretty "skilled" husband, it took him two and a half seconds and one look at my face to say, "I'm sorry, that was bad, wasn't it?" We actually both had a good laugh over it and chalked it up to the differences in how men and women think. But, without this insight, could you see how hurtful and damaging this could be to the relationship?

The biggest mistake a man can make is to try to be a rational problem-solver or to convince his wife not to feel how she feels in the moment she is expressing her feelings about being stressed or upset. Seems like the logical thing to do, right, fellas? But remember, husbands—write it on your hand, your heart, and your forehead if necessary—she needs your emotional **comfort** and to be told that she is normal, not a reminder that her suffering is her "own fault" or that she has "issues." We already hear that in our heads from the Enemy on a daily basis. So you can be on God's side, speaking truth, or you can be accompanying the "Great Accuser" as a voice of discouragement and rejection in her mind.

Men will never completely understand the battle women have in their heads and in their hearts because of our emotions, but our husband's efforts to understand us go a long, long way. Something that takes a man a moment to do, such as make a decision, for-give, plan for the future, or deal with a stressful situation, would take a woman a million thoughts, options, and possibilities along with all the **tragic** outcomes in our mind that can cause us to be emotional for hours or even days. If our husbands can help make us feel secure and reassure us that we are not crazy or broken, but that we are a beautiful gift from God, despite our negative emo-tional times, and even say they appreciate that we are the emo-tional ones (I know it seems like crazy-talk, but take my word for it), they will see a beautiful, thriving wife appear that will admit she is well-loved by her husband and thereby, eventually, because of those efforts, is less emotional. This scenario, my dear friends, will create one heck of a strong emotional bond between husband and wife. Frankly, gentlemen, it is your insurance policy, because if you can emotionally care for us in our times of "craziness," we can forgive you and your "dumb-guy" incidents every single day of the week!

Review

- The deeper and more intimately a husband understands his wife, the healthier and happier she will be.
- Husbands, rediscover her favorite things.
- A good, strong hug from a husband can make his wife feel safe, loved, and reassured; that she can trust her husband; and that he can make her feel like everything will be ok when her mind and emotions tell her otherwise.
- Not allowing walls to be built within the marital relationship is the responsibility of both the man and the woman and both must work hard to have resolution to feelings, conflict, and past hurts and wounds to have a healthy marriage.
- Husbands need to take on responsibility in areas that cause

their wives stress and worry, because God created them to do it.

- Women desperately need the approval and validation of their husbands to know they are loved for exactly who they are, not that their husband's love is contingent on how they need to change or improve.
- If men can take on the role of emotional caregiver for their wives, the marriage will be significantly improved and it will be evident in the peace and overall well-being of his wife.

∗ ∗ ∗

A Prayer for Husbands

Dear Father in Heaven,

Fill me with the power and wisdom of the Holy Spirit in the ways that I can be an emotional caregiver to my wife. Help me, Lord Jesus, in every step of the way. Help me to be a hero, a father, a romantic, and an expert in communication and to treat her like the beauty I pursued the day I asked her to marry me. I bless my wife to be healthy and thriving mentally, emotionally, and spiritually. I choose to be a leader in the important areas of her life. I hereby choose to be loving and considerate of her emotions and learn how to make my wife feel like a priority and deeply cherished by me, on a daily basis. Fill me with the wisdom and the motivation to be these roles for my wife. I care for her deeply and want her to know and believe how precious she is to me.

I pray this in the name of my Lord and Savior, Jesus Christ. Amen.

4

The Horror Show in My Head

"Women process life more like a plate of pasta. If you look at a plate of spaghetti, you notice there are lots of individual noodles that all touch one another. If you attempt to follow one noodle around the plate, you will intersect a lot of other noodles, and you might even switch to another noodle seamlessly. Women face life in this way. Every thought and issue is connected to every other thought and issue in some way. Life is much more of a process for women than it is for men."
—Bill and Pam Farrel, *Men Are Like Waffles, Women Are Like Spaghetti*

The title of this chapter, "The Horror Show in My Head," came from this real-life situation and conversation that occurred between me and my husband. I was trying to describe to my husband the mental-emotional struggles that women typically endure, in hopes that he would better understand me, but also to enable him to have insight and be able to give this wisdom to the other husbands he counsels. We were in the midst of miscommunication and conflict. We were equally frustrated with each other, suffering from the common differences in our male and female brains, which were complicated by the inability to effectively communicate our perspectives. Out of frustration, Scott said something like, "I just don't understand why you **have** to feel that way. It is not rational or helpful. Just decide to not feel that way." The response I had in my head I will not put into print, but the "nicer" version sounded something like, "I would **love** to just **not** think or feel upset and just change my emotions with ease!" With wisdom, and in an attempt to still be somewhat respectful, I said, "I do not **want** to feel this way, but I cannot seem to get these upsetting thoughts or radical emotions within me to stop **making** me feel upset." I then followed that up with, "There is a horror show in my head, constantly filled with thoughts, feelings, fears, and assumptions, and you, my dear, do **not** want to be,"—as I pointed to my brain—"in here!" At that point, we both laughed and, believe it or not, it gave us both a new perspective about how women think and feel. This new perspective also helps wives feel validated about their emotions and to help husbands have a mental picture of what it must be like for their wives internally, when externally all they see are emotional "psychopaths" **being upset over "nothing."** (I hate it when my husband says that. It surely does not seem like **"nothing"** to wives.)

Every woman can understand and sympathize with what I am talking about; at times, we can be very reasonable, rational, and intelligent women, and yet we cannot seem to talk ourselves out of our doubts, fears, and irrational emotions. Every woman has had the horrifying and exhausting experience of trying to make out a simple grocery list and by the time you have written "milk, bread and eggs" you have had 1.2 million other thoughts ranging from "where did I put those coupons" to "which candidate will I vote for in the next presidential term" to "I wonder what my daughter will be when she grows up?"

No joke. It's ridiculously impossible for us to have just one thought at a time. The opening quote of this chapter (from *Men Are Like Waffles and Women Are Like Spaghetti* by Bill and Pam Farrell) is a great visual and a wonderful book that can help give us a great mental picture of a woman's emotional thought process. Men can compartmentalize their thoughts and focus on one thing at a time, like the little squares of a waffle, which typically is less anxiety-ridden and more effective in logical thinking. Women, on the other hand, think of many different things at once that are all interconnected, which allows us to be multitasking and very aware of our surroundings, but also creating stress and mental chaos in our minds, like a pile of noodles!

I encourage men in couples counseling, "Have compassion for your wife. You will never really understand what it is like to have the thoughts, feelings, and emotions she does, so all you can do is be grateful your brain does not operate this way (which usually gets a laugh) and offer her grace and forgiveness when she thinks, acts, and talks like she is losing it!" This is where the notion of "women are crazy," from a man's perspective, comes from—because of how women act and react in their relationships and within the world around them.

The Crazy Continuum

I want to offer two explanations to husbands and wives for why women experience the super-emotional "crazy" feeling: scientific and spiritual.

The scientific explanation is that men's and women's brains biologically function differently. A man's thoughts typically run more from front to back on each side of the brain, switching from his left to right hemisphere depending on if he needs to be problem-solving or whether he needs to deal with more emotionally based issues. This would suggest that men are likely to be more definitively right-brained (more intuitive) or left-brained (more logical) than women, depending on if they spend more time in one hemisphere or the other. Women's brains are more likely to use both hemispheres at once or quickly communicate back and forth between intuitive and logical which allows them to be multi-tasking, relational, emotional, and logical, but this also lends itself to making women feel emotional, anxious, overwhelmed and, well . . . **"nuts!"** (No, that is not a clinical term. Husbands, you can **never, ever** use that phrase with your wives.)

The spiritual explanation is that there is good and evil in this world. If you believe there is a God in Heaven, then you must acknowledge there is an Enemy against us: Satan. With that being said, Satan makes attempts every day to affect men and women in ways that will keep them from living a joyful, victorious life. Why does he do this, you might ask? He wants to prevent us from living a life full of glory and gratitude to God for our gift of eternal life. The Enemy wants to use fears, doubt, stress, worry, and sin of all kinds to keep us distracted and in bondage. I use the word "attacked" as a description of the ways Satan tries to ruin our life. He does so by telling us lies in our mind, accusing us of the mistakes we have made in the past, and reminding us of the awful things people have said or done to hurt us. Men are "attacked" mostly in the ways of being emasculated, such as: you are weak, inadequate, and worthless. Women, on the other hand, are attacked in our thoughts and feelings, such as: you are unlovable, not valuable, and not good enough. With these predisposed thoughts and assumptions constantly running through our minds, veins, and our whole being as a wife, our husbands can hurt us pretty easily, and wives can hit a man's disrespect button fairly quickly. Add to that equation the stress of the outside world making women feel completely emotional and, yup, you guessed it, **crazy**. I have had so many women ask me over the years, "Am I crazy?" We have all seen comedians and sitcoms poke fun at the idea that women are crazy, so I began to paradoxically go along with it for the sake of validating women. My explanation to them is that we, as women, are all on a **crazy continuum**. Some days are pretty good and we might be only a one or a two on a scale of one to ten, but on days when our husbands are insensitive and our kids are out of control, we might be a nine or ten. But this scale is meant to bring a little light humor to a very difficult and frustrating situation for women. I reassure women it is still just a "feeling" and really a mistaken belief; women are not crazy. Wives will never be able to completely shut off their emotions, at least not in a healthy way, so accepting times when we feel overwhelmed and learning to express ourselves effectively is a very good goal.

I have been a professional counselor for fifteen years. I have attended a hundred seminars and have read several hundred self-help and clinical psychology books, and I have found no magical, therapeutic technique that will transform a woman's emotional struggles into perfectly logical, rational thoughts. Rather, I have learned, it is more helpful to accept the fact that God has made us to be emotional for a reason, and we should stop trying to be something we are not. We are not always logical, rational, cyborgs with a computer chip that controls our emotions. With this realization and spiritual wisdom, women can begin to build on their strengths of being emotionally savvy, nurturing, and compassionate; learn how to submit our weaknesses to God; and they will naturally begin to thrive and flourish in life.

I am hoping this explanation is freeing for many women; freeing them from their self-condemnation or judgment of others. You are **not** crazy, and please stop calling other women crazy. When you feel the overwhelming emotions and the thought comes into your head that there is something wrong with you, you can just say, "God has made me an emotional being, and, therefore, I will call on Him to help me through this." Women were designed to be emotional creatures, and we will never achieve perfection in managing our emotions and restraining our reactions to our inner feelings with perfect behavior. Although this is not an excuse for ungodly thoughts or behaviors, we must learn to take unhealthy, ungodly thoughts and lies from the Enemy captive. Everyone, man or woman, must sacrifice their **instinctual** reactions to thoughts and feelings and apply truth and wisdom to their lives. Through biblical teachings and good Christian counsel, women must continue to make an effort to rise above their negativity and panic.

> "The weapons of our warfare are not of the flesh but have divine power to destroy strongholds. We destroy arguments and every lofty opinion raised against the knowledge of God, and take every thought captive to obey Christ."
> —2 Corinthians 10:4–5

This information on the radical thoughts and emotions in the minds of your wives might be completely new to some of you men. Others of you might be scratching your head or rubbing your chin and making "aha" sounds. Others have heard or read these types of things before but they continue to not express the empathy or compassion wives so desperately need. In fact, many men have not accepted the truth that this emotional component in women is simply how God made them and wives will never "be emotionless and just think more like men." Many men struggle with irrational and emotional thoughts at times, too. Applying the advice to take negative, ungodly thoughts captive is excellent counsel for men and women alike. Further advice on how to battle these thoughts is found later is this chapter.

A quick disclaimer: This does not mean that as wives, we can have unreasonable expectations of our husbands now that they have some understanding of how we "tick." Because we are so differently compromised biologically, physically, and emotionally, women need to seek additional healthy resources other than our spouse in order to meet our many emotional needs. As we would like our husbands to have a deeper understanding and empathy for our mental and emotional battle, we should have patience, tolerance, and forgiveness for them in times when they are trying to be loving and caring but perhaps are falling short. It is very easy in the moment that we are in need of emotional care and perhaps have been in desperate need of it for a while to react harshly and disrespectfully to our spouse. God has called us to respect our husbands and that is something that takes restraint, talent, and it requires wives to be in agreement with the belief that this is a Godly behavior and role they want to take on, believing it will help us thrive within our marriages.

Husbands and wives will have less conflict, fewer resentments, and a stronger, more fulfilling marriage if they can simply accept each other for the way they are and truly make an effort to see each other through the eyes of Christ, which is loved, accepted, and valuable no matter what their failures. And yes, you have to continue to tell your husband what you need. I ask wives to take on the role as the relationship expert in the marriage; it is truly more natural for you. Women are usually better at communication and better at sensing emotions in others and in ourselves, and we are usually the ones with hidden resentments or unmet needs, thus we need to fight and advocate for those needs to protect the emotional connection in the marriage. With a strong emotional connection, consistent conflict resolution, and increased respectful communication with your spouse, you will enjoy your marriage more than you ever thought was possible.

An Enemy Against Us

One of the most crucial pieces of wisdom I want to share in this chapter is not to offer further explanation of the female brain to men, nor to validate the feelings of women so they do not feel crazy (although these are valid and important points). Rather, it is how women can **stop** the horror show in our heads. The Bible says the battle of life is not here on earth, but in our minds against evil forces (paraphrased Ephesians 6:10-17). As a counselor, this is one piece of Scripture I discuss and educate my clients about often, because it holds a valuable explanation as to why we think negative thoughts. It also gives us the key to being set free from such thoughts.

Step One: Recognize there is an Enemy against us. Satan will always use our strengths against us and twist them into our weaknesses in attempt to convince us to abandon them. With that being said, how would this sneaky little devil attack us women? The Enemy can destroy women through the intensity of our emotions and in our minds. Our love, passion, and emotions are our greatest God-given strengths, but Satan can make us feel weak by using emotions such as worry and concern to drive up strife in our lives. Ladies, do you ever have those ridiculous thoughts of your husband dying or your children getting hurt and you are not there to comfort them? And then you start crying just thinking about it? Or worse yet, if something happened to you, and your kids were left for your husband to take care of? (Husbands, don't be offended; it's not that you wouldn't do a good job. It's just that all women feel **no one** can care for and love their children like a mother.)

We know as Christian wives and mothers we "shouldn't" worry

or have fear, but many of us just do not know how to turn those emotions off. The first step is recognizing most of these thoughts are not your own; they are simply good, well-intended affection gone awry. Satan doesn't want us living free to love everyone around us or to be caring and compassionate effectively! He wants to mess with us, all day and probably all night. As long as Satan can continue to stir up negative emotions in us, we are kept from being the best we can be. In theory, most women are excited and looking forward to spending time with their husbands or children, but then the first chance they have to interact with their loved ones, out of stress and frustration, they end up wanting to rip their heads off, rather than hug and kiss them. This is because the female brain can be both optimistic and have fantasy-like expectations, and then she can be devastated and disappointed when things do not go well.

Step Two: Men and women need to recognize that a great deal of stress and anxiety comes from the need to be in control. It is easy to say we realize we are not in control; God is. But it is much harder to turn off our emotions so that we can actually rest and have peace in the knowledge that "God's got it." One thing that has helped me is making a daily prayer that God protects my mind from such attacks. I also pray He gives me the insight and wisdom as to when I start to become emotional or lose joy due to unhealthy or ungodly feelings so I can correct it with His promises and truth. This has changed my stress and anxiety level tremendously. The basic prayer I use is found at the end of this chapter.

Step Three: It is important for women to realize their feelings are real, normal, and valid. But a wise and healthy woman will also acknowledge when these feelings are hurtful, unhealthy, and causing problems for her, and she will instead strive for balance in her life.

One example is how upset we can become about our husband's annoying habits. Underwear on the bathroom floor, leaving his dishes in the sink, doesn't ask what others want to watch on TV . . . etc. We all have the "list." No matter what it might be, the more we fixate on it, try to have unreasonable expectations about it, or allow ourselves to become worked up about it, the truth is that we can be annoying too. Not me, of course, but I'm sure most other women are. I'm kidding. In fact, one time after some painful self-reflection, I told my husband one of his greatest strengths as a husband was his ability to "put up with me." So, in other words, we need to have forgiveness for our husbands' shortcomings, choose to throw out the list of what we think we **deserve**, and be Christ-like servants in the marriage. Giving in to Satan's attempts to attack us can cause us emotional pain and angry or bitter feelings towards our spouse. Some women might say, "But you don't know just how annoying or neglectful my husband can be." My answer is somewhat harsh, but it is accurate: "It doesn't matter." We are called as a spouse to serve and sacrifice for our partner, to give up our needs and rights like Jesus did for us on the cross. It sounds like a tall order, but honestly, the more you **choose** to do it, the less anger, hurt, and frustration you will have. Then there is the bonus of your spouse noticing the difference in you, and it will improve your emotional connection with him—which is worth a lifetime of picking up his underwear. When I counsel women about this role in their marriage I tell them this: You can wake up every morning and say towards Heaven, "Lord I am Your child and servant. Everything I do today, I pray it pleases you. I want to be a blessing to my spouse and my children." Then when you go to pick up the laundry, do the dishes, and sit through another episode of that car renovation show your husband always watches, you can pleasantly chant in your head, *I am a blessing* *and I choose to do this with joy because God is pleased with me!* I will admit, it takes some practice and there are some days where it will be hard to "feel" the joy, but it is worth the effort. You will have more peace and a happier mood, and your husband will feel close to you because you do not nag him or withdraw from him because of your secret resentments towards him.

Wives: Our mental, emotional, and spiritual health is OUR responsibility. Yes, your past has a part in it, yes hurts and wounds matter, but there is healing in Christ. There are many excellent Christian counselors and resources that can offer wise counsel on how to relieve your negative thinking, and I urge you to seek additional wisdom and education in this area if you have never done so. Some of my favorite female writers that have inspired me are Joyce Meyers, Beth Moore, Elizabeth George, Stormie Omartian, Lysa TerKeurst, and Angela Thomas, just to name a few. Wise women do not blame their past or other people for their pain or emotional well-being, rather they ask God for healing and seek the wisdom and resources that will help them along a healthier path.

Review

- The way women think is different than how men think. Neither sex is wrong—just created to think differently, and we need to remember to appreciate that about one another rather than criticize it.
- Our spouse is not the enemy; Satan is.
- Managing emotions involve having spiritual wisdom, skills, and prayer.
- There is peace and comfort in knowing God is in control and you can trust Him.
- Women cannot be without emotions, but they can learn how

be healthy in getting their needs met, which will leave them healthier in their marriage and with their overall life satisfaction.

* * *

Prayer for Physical, Mental, and Emotional Health

Dear Father God,

I call on the power and authority given to me by becoming a child of God and accepting Jesus as my Savior in all that I encounter today. I believe Jesus is the King of kings and is seated at the right hand of the Father. I believe that Jesus has victory over Satan and all the enemies of Christ, therefore I am seated at the right hand of Jesus, and all Satan's schemes against me are beneath my feet. I have power and victory through forgiveness by the blood of Jesus and receive renewal and healing through the dunamis power of the resurrection of our Lord and Savior, Jesus Christ.

Please forgive me for my sins today. I ask that if there is anything specifically I did to others or myself in thought, action, or emotion that was not pleasing to You that You remind me of it, so I may confess it now. (Take a moment to be silent and hear from Jesus.) I ask for forgiveness for hurting others with my thoughts or words, my selfishness, or lack of concern.

I ask for forgiveness for speaking any curses over the lives of those I encountered today and rebuke them now in the name of Jesus Christ my Lord and Savior. I rebuke and command that all curses be broken that were spoken over my life or the life of my family/children today, and do so by ap-

plying them to the blood of Jesus, who sacrificed His life so that I may be set free from condemnation, curses, and sin.

I cancel all judgments made against me falsely or unintentionally by others or by myself. I ask for forgiveness for believing Satan's lies and not Your Truth, Lord Jesus Christ. I pray to submit my will each day to you Lord and ask that you continue to point me in the way that is righteous and obedient to You. I want to align my will with Yours and no one else's.

I ask that anything unhealthy I have put into my mind, will, emotions, heart, body, or breath today be cleansed by You and dispensed from by body, mind, will, and spirit forever through the powerful healing of the resurrection and how the sacrifice of Your Son conquers and redeems all death, evil, or darkness in my life. Make my body renewed in You and allow it to be healed of disease, dysfunction, curse, generational sin, or any biological dysfunction. I claim victory over all earthly, human issues with my body, mind, soul, or emotions and ask You to open the Heavenly realms, rain down Your Glory, and restore me fully to the person and the spirit you made me to be the day you created me in my mother's womb.

I ask You Father God to send a legion of Warrior-Army angels to protect me from all evil and any attempts legally, illegally, or otherwise that Satan and his army of darkness might try to use to come against me or my family. I stand firm in faith, Your Word, and my eternal life through Jesus in all encounters with evil today, protect and guide me in this battle. I submit my will and life to you Lord, today and always.

In Jesus's name,

Amen.

5

The Unconditional Love You've Been Looking For

Ancient Greek acknowledges Four Types of Love:
Philos Love *is the unique kind of love you have for a friend, brother, or sister; this is the kind of love Christians tend to show towards one another.* ***Eros Love*** *is the type of desire and longing we have for our spouse in a marriage. It can tend to be selfish and liable to die out over time if it does not involve the presence of the Lord.* ***Storge Love*** *is the common or natural empathy felt by parents for their children and refers to mere tolerance and acceptance.* ***Agape Love*** *is the special term for the divine love God has for His Son, human beings, and all believers.*

Many husbands and wives have said over the years, "I wish my spouse would just love me unconditionally." Even in individual counseling, many people's childhood hurts and wounds lead back to **not** feeling unconditionally loved or accepted by their parents. In this chapter, you will learn the truth, which is that we all need to feel unconditionally loved in order to have hope that we are valuable, considered worthy of love, and good enough for someone to love. The fact is, only God can truly love unconditionally.

As long as we are human, we are weak and will eventually fall to our weaknesses, which will affect and hurt those around us. Having an expectation of our parents, our spouses, our children, and especially of ourselves to love unconditionally is just, well, ridiculous.

This chapter will also help address the kind of love we are called to give as a human beings and that this kind of love is difficult to follow through on, and it will never really be the **unconditional** kind of love we receive from God. We can speak out of frustration, hurt, or anger, and at times we can lash out at others out of defensiveness, pride, or grief. We can begin to shut down or self-protect if we have felt hurt by our loved ones too severely or for too long. It is not in our human nature to love perfectly or unconditionally.

The way we should **strive** to love one another is found in the Scripture almost everyone uses at their wedding ceremony:

> *"Love is patient and kind; love does not envy or boast; it is not arrogant or rude. It does not insist on its own way; it is not irritable or resentful; it does not rejoice at wrongdoing, but rejoices with the truth. Love bears all things, believes all things, hopes all things, endures all things."*
> *—I Corinthians 13:4–7*

Meditate and truly comprehend how tremendous the outline of this kind of radical love is; we are called to have **this kind of love** for our spouse. Love is patient. (I'm toast already!) Love is kind. Love is not jealous. Love is not proud and does not **boast**. (Even if you did the dishes every night this week.) Love does not do things that are not nice. Love does not just think of itself. Love does not get angry. Love holds no wrong feeling in the heart. (Even if he forgot your birthday.) Love is not glad when people do wrong things. (Even though it completely proves all your negative assumptions about your spouse, which can feel validating). But it is always glad when they do right. Love forgives **everything**. (Yup, there is that word **forgiveness** again.) Love is always trusting, is always hoping, and **never gives up!**

We definitely have our work cut out for us, and surely we will fall short by this definition of love, but focus on the specific areas in which **you** could improve. Know you are not loving your family, friends, or spouse perfectly, and that is ok. Only God has perfect love for us. Really, the best we can do is to try to see our loved ones through God's eyes, knowing and believing how much HE loves them, and perhaps we can have just a small glimpse of how to love them, despite the ways they disappoint or hurt us. Trying to see ourselves through His eyes is also a wonderful revelation of the immense love God has for us. It is such an intense and all-encompassing love. I truly believe it is beyond our comprehension until we go home to meet Him someday.

I believe each of us has a strong desire to be loved unconditionally because it is a craving placed in us by our Creator, but without a spiritual awakening and surrender to Him, we will walk to the ends of this earth looking and yearning for love and always feeling disappointed with the "hole in our soul." Many people seek to fill their emptiness with achievements, success, a spouse, having children, buying things, eating delicious foods, and going on vacations, but at the end of the day they are still not really **fulfilled**. If you have this desire and have felt continually let down by your parents, friends, or spouse to feel truly loved in a way that completes you, I urge you to consider inviting Jesus Christ to fill this space. If this is something you have yet to do and would like to feel God's complete and perfect love, say the following prayer aloud. If you mean the words as you say them and believe them to be true, you will gain eternal life in Heaven and forever be the beloved child of the most loving and affectionate Father God. Your life will be transformed, you will no longer be just flesh and blood, but born of the Spirit of God.

Dear Father God,

I come to You right now and ask You to fill me up with Your love through the power of the Holy Spirit, so that I may experience becoming a part of Your Holy and Righteous Family. I believe that You sent Your son Jesus to die for me and set me free from all iniquity of sin, curse, or judgment. Please forgive me for all my sins and apply the blood of Jesus to these sins, which was shed for me on the cross. I believe the blood of Jesus covers all of my sins from the past, the present, and the ones I have yet to commit. I acknowledge you are the Creator, Father God, and praise you for the beautiful work You have done in me. I ask to know You more deeply and intimately. I want to relentlessly experience a true and perfect love with Jesus, my Lord and Savior. I want to rely only on You, surrender my life to You, and ask You to lead my life. I will depend only on You for all my needs. Thank You for loving me unconditionally and creating me exactly the way You intended me to be, with gifts and a purpose, which I now intend to use for Your glory and Your kingdom.

In Jesus's name I pray.

Amen.

I would encourage all Christians, new to faith or those that are more mature in knowledge and wisdom, to seek out Scripture in the Bible as to how much God loves us. Understanding Him and

His character will help you realize how much He truly does love you. Soaking in this revelation daily will keep you from doubt, fear, loneliness, and looking to others—especially your spouse—for the kind of love you can only receive from your Father in Heaven. Ever hear people say someone has "daddy issues"? It usually refers to the fact that person is having some kind of dysfunctional behavior or emotional issues caused by not being loved or accepted by their father. The same is true of God. Without an intimate and loving relationship with Him, your life will always be somewhat dysfunctional and you will miss out on the most amazing, constant and overwhelming love you could ever imagine. The more you understand His perfect love for you, the stronger of mind you will be, the less offended by others you will feel, and the more capable you will be to selflessly give love to others.

Why Are We Always So Desperately Seeking Love?

If we do not tap into the spiritual part of us, we have only human, earthly expectations in life, and we will most definitely be gravely disappointed about how we are loved. If you are willing to look at the spiritual side of life and if you are going to understand this question about unconditional love better, you need to understand what causes us to believe we are **not** loved. Well, just as there is a God in Heaven and He is a good and faithful force, there is also evil; Satan is called the "great accuser" and the father of all liars (John 8:44). From the onset of our childhood he is on the prowl, the Bible says, "like a lion ready to devour us" (1 Peter 5:8). The way Satan tries to destroy our confidence and ability to do great things for God's kingdom is to have us believe lies in our head that would make us feel rejected and unloved. Many young men and women did not grow up feeling enough love or approval from their parents. Without this first valuable foundation in a young person's life, it leaves a wide-open wound for Satan to attack men and women to convince them they are not loved. This will happen from the time we are young children, through our teen years, and especially within our marriages.

The most common lies from the Enemy that a man will believe about himself are that he is weak, inadequate, or a failure. Perhaps as a young man he felt approval from his parents but harshly rejected by his first girlfriend or, even worse, his wife. It might even be a friend, boss, or mentor who made him feel like a failure. Whatever the wound, Satan will use it to make you question whether you are truly deserving of unconditional love. Soon, a man begins to rationalize in unhealthy ways, "I have screwed up a lot, I am not that important, I haven't really achieved anything that great," and so on. Poor self-confidence in feeling approval or unconditional love for a man leads to many relationship issues, anger, poor self-esteem, as well as physical sickness and disease later in life.

You will **never be perfectly** loved by the humans around you, "loved ones" or not. You will, at some point, be offended, hurt and rejected in some way by them. But with the deep love, affection, and irreversible acceptance by God, you can handle the rejection of others and still be strong and confident against Satan's attempts to lie to you. When Satan tries to come against a man who is firmly rooted in God's love and tries to make him feel defeated, the believer will simply react in this way: "I am righteous because of Jesus." When the Father of Lies whispers, "you are a failure and worthless and have accomplished nothing," you can stand on God's promises that the "work" has already been done in you by Him. You will always have approval and be a success in the eyes of our Heavenly Father, and when the Evil One shouts, "You are weak, full of fear and you will never be good enough," you can cry out with confidence: "I am not afraid, God is my rock (Psalm 27:1), and He will uphold me in His mighty hand, and I can do all things through Christ, who strengthens me (Philippians 4:13)."

For women, our need for unconditional love is similar. It is a deep desire put in us by God to yearn for the intimate and profoundly holy relationship He would like to have with us. Seeking unconditional love from our husband, father, or friend will usually leave us feeling not good enough, like we are unlovable and not worthy. Women who do not experience God's great love and approval for them can suffer from eating disorders, self-image issues, depression, anxiety, and an unhealthy dependence on men. But through understanding how much God loves us, a woman can be firmly rooted in the fact that when God see us, all He sees is the beauty He created in us. We cannot divert His love for us, and we can never make enough mistakes for Him to stop loving us. We are also perfect in His eyes, not because we are great or because we try hard, but because He sees Jesus in us. This would be a helpful concept for some women to acknowledge for themselves; the goodness and perfection of Christ **is** within us when we invite Him into our hearts. When women understand these truths, they will never have poor self-esteem again. God loves you perfectly, and you are made perfect in His love.

I would advise every reader of this: Review 1 Corinthians 13:4-7 often as a reminder and as a guide of the love that we can strive to give and be for others, but know we will fail, in our efforts, as others will fail us. We are only human and cannot give, accept, or express love perfectly. In those times that we or others fall short, turn to God to fulfill your need for love, for He is truly the only one who can do it unconditionally. Have grace and forgiveness for yourself and others for doing the best they can to be loving towards you. It is also very important to read the Bible, listen to worship music, and read Father-focused devotionals that help you understand God's character and nature of His love to truly grasp how much **He loves you**.

What We Truly Need in A Marriage Is Covenant Love

The definition of covenant love is one that is an unbreakable promise, a bond, and a guarantee that you will love one another until the day you die. This kind of love is not a "feeling" but a commitment of one's will. When your spouse seems "unlovable," that is the time to ask God to protect your marriage and heal the brokenness between the two of you. It requires putting effort into forgiveness and seeing your loved ones through the eyes of Christ. This kind of love cannot "die out" or just fade away. In the many years I have been facilitating marriage counseling, probably the most common complaint is that one or both of the spouses "just aren't in love with each other anymore." This cannot happen with covenant love.

An example of a "covenant" would be a lease or mortgage on your house. It is a signed deed and contract, and once it is signed there is a commitment to make a monthly payment. We cannot simply say, "I'm just not feeling it this month . . ." Not paying the mortgage comes with some very serious consequences, as does giving up on your covenant to love and cherish your spouse, until death do you part. The romantic love we see in movies is impossible to find, or at least impossible to maintain. Couples who have been married for more than a few months know that it takes some work and effort to resolve conflict and forgive and appreciate one another. Walks on the beach, picnics, and make-out sessions in the car are few and far between, especially when you have children. But these are not bad things to desire and pursue; romance is fun and nourishes and enhances a covenant love, but romance without the covenant will always run out. Another unhealthy expectation in marriage is to expect to have the passionate love we experience the first year or two we are together.

Notice I said the first year or two we are "together"? Many people joke that as soon as a couple becomes married the passion dies. There are a couple explanations for that: First, most people are on their best behavior the first year and even into the second year of being together. Most of us can somewhat "mask" the more difficult or wounded parts of ourselves, especially if the couple is not living together. Second, passionate love is often actually just lust. Lust is the kind of feeling we get through the temptation of sexual sin. Having sexual contact in **any way** with our spouse-to-be will cause us to have feelings towards each other sexually and creates a bond that God intended to **only** happen between husband and wife as a very special gift to connect us to one another. The gift of a sexual relationship is Godly ordained that a married couple would be bonded in a way that would be unlike any other human relationship in our life.

When this "bond" happens outside the sacrament of marriage, it becomes ungodly and lustful. Then when the couple becomes married and the sexual relationship is now blessed, "lust" feelings leave. But then couples might feel like when the sexual sin of lust leaves, so does the passion in their relationship, because it was what they recognized as love and the emotional connection they were feeling toward one another. Whether you are not yet married, or are married, or remarried and you did have sexual relationships outside of marriage, I strongly encourage you to pray the prayer to break soul ties at the end of chapter thirteen. I have had many counseling experiences in which a couple was having issues with emotional closeness, inability to forgive one another, affairs, or sexual dysfunction of some kind. After praying the prayer to break soul ties, they were immediately relieved of those issues and their marriage—especially the sexual relationship—began to flourish and thrive.

The "false" kinds of love presented above are all a lie, an illusion sold to us by the world, orchestrated by the Enemy to make us give up on our marriage or at least continue to live miserably in an unfulfilling marriage. When most of us decided to marry, we were asked to commit to one another until **death do us part**. That means we made a **covenant** to love one another, only breakable by death. I understand that sounds a little extreme, but that is God's heart for marriage. There are very unhealthy and even dangerous people and dysfunctional marriages in which I believe God gives authority to end the marriage, and that person can still live a blessed life. But I also believe that if a couple knew the true understanding of what covenant love was from the beginning of their marriage, it would change the future of many marriages.

Review

- Eros love: marital love.
- Philos love: brotherly love.
- Storge love: parent's love for their child.
- Agape love: divine love from God.
- We all need unconditional love from our Heavenly Father to be healthy physically, emotionally and spiritually.
- Covenant love is what makes a marriage last.
- Romantic love, passionate love, and lust are false expectations of what "true love" is in a marriage that will lead to feelings of dissatisfaction and hopelessness in the marriage.

Instead of a prayer, I would offer you the following wedding vows, and ask you as a couple to "renew" your vows, aloud, before each other, with a renewed sense of commitment. It is important that both spouses are willing and motivated to make these vows with earnest and sincere dedication. Some couples have even recognized the importance and value of this covenant and they have chosen to make it a family ceremony to celebrate it and declare it before others.

* * *

Male

I, _____, take you, _____, to be my wedded wife. With deepest joy, I receive you into my life that together we may be one. As is Christ to His body, the church, so I will be to you a loving and faithful husband. Always will I perform my headship over you even as Christ does over me, knowing that His Lordship is one of the holiest desires for my life. I promise you my deepest love, my fullest devotion, and my most tender care. I promise I will live first unto God rather than others or even you. I promise that I will lead our lives into a life of faith and hope in Christ Jesus, ever honoring God's guidance by His spirit through the Word. And so throughout life, no matter what may lie ahead of us, I pledge to you my life as a loving and faithful husband.

Female

I, _____, take you, _____, to be my wedded husband. With deepest joy, I come into my new life with you. As you have pledged to me your life and love, so I too happily give you my life, and in confidence submit myself to your headship as to the Lord. As is the church in her relationship to Christ, so I will be to you. _____, I will live first unto our God and then unto you, loving you, obeying you, caring for you and ever seeking to please you. God has prepared me for you and so I will ever strengthen, help, comfort, and encourage you. Therefore, throughout life, no matter what may be ahead of us, I pledge to you my life as a submitted and faithful wife.

—Adapted from Bible.org

6

Code Readers

*Gary: You **just** said that you want me to help you do the dishes.*

*Brooke: I want you to **want** to do the dishes.*

Gary: Why would I want to do dishes?

Brooke: Why? See, that's my whole point.

Gary: Let me see if I'm following this, ok? Are you telling me that you're upset because I don't have a strong desire to clean dishes?

Brooke: No. I'm upset because you don't have a strong desire to offer to do the dishes.

Gary: I just did.

Brooke: After I asked you!

—Vince Vaughn and Jennifer Aniston in *The Break-Up*

Husbands, did anyone explain to you at the marriage altar that you would be required to be expert espionage code-readers and need to have the intellectual capacity of a rocket scientist in order to meet the needs of your wives? That is the conclusion many men come to believe about being able to please their wives within the marriage after a few years into the relationship. Almost every husband comes to hear the silent message of failure, and he can become very overwhelmed and hopeless. All joking aside, it is a crucial part of your job as a husband to make your wife feel completely understood and secure in the marital relationship through active listening, validation, and good communication. Those of you who have been married for more than a few days know that this is a far greater feat than was ever imagined in those "fun and easy" days of dating.

So often what a man will hear from his wife is this: "Why don't you try to understand me. You don't get it. You just really don't care, do you?" And if she doesn't express this verbally, she is thinking it. A woman gains her sense of worth and importance and of being valued by her husband through his ability to understand her and make her feel validated in her emotions. I have heard from many men that we counsel, as well as out of the lips of my own husband, "How can you not know that I love you?" Well, the answer to that question is very simple for women . . . in "female-land," we understand exactly what we need and how we would like it said, the facial expression we would like to see, the intentional actions and the small, yet thoughtful, gift that would go along with it! Ha, just kidding about the gift, fellas. (Although, gifts never hurt.)

It is easier for the analytical, logical brain of a man to jump to solutions, and the husband can become frustrated when **his** rationale is not working on his wife. Many men I have counseled will state something like, "I need a rule-book for my wife; if I just knew exactly what to do or say, I would do it." The problem with that solution, gentlemen, is that your wife's feelings change on a daily basis. Circumstances, stress, hormones, being tired, illness, and any "ole" reason could affect "what" your wife needs. Sometimes a woman doesn't even understand how she feels or knows what she needs. Then how are husbands supposed to know what she needs, you might say? Starting to sound hopeless? Not at all.

The good news is that your job is much simpler than being an international spy trying to break foreign tactical codes. Just listen and follow these easy steps:

Ask your wife **often** how she is doing. That does NOT mean you say, "What is your problem?" or "What is wrong with you?" when she seems upset. After knowing her for more than a couple of months, you will know by her response if you need to continue to ask her questions or actually give her some space. Do not be afraid of her answer or fear the ensuing conflict, for this is exactly the time she **needs** you, her husband, the most. If she is cheerful or appears lighthearted and says, "I'm fine," then she is really fine. But if she seems tired, sad, upset, or lacking joy in any way and says, "I'm fine," she is not ok. Why do we do this? For a couple reasons, and it actually depends a lot on the woman's temperament. One temperament type is so busy thinking about how she feels in her head that she has a difficult time putting it into words. One type does not like to be that vulnerable with her emotions. Another type wants to be pursued vigorously and wants you to ask a lot of questions and even "guess" at how she is feeling, which makes your effort and whether you really care about her seem more genuine. Some wives might be pretty good at telling you how they feel; but, in an effort to not overwhelm you with her emotions, she might say she's fine and wait for you to ask more questions to be sure you are ready and have the time for the whirlwind of thoughts and feelings that will be coming your way.

When your wife is upset, frustrated, or even hostile, keep reminding yourself she is in need of emotional care from you. Your wife does not intend for this to be a volcanic attack of molten word vomit onto you. She is simply in desperate need of comfort from the one person who can soothe her better than anyone else: you, her husband. A woman desires to intimately connect to her husband emotionally, intellectually, and spiritually. Sharing our daily frustrations, internal thoughts, and emotions (as psychotic as they might seem) is our way of connecting to our husbands on a deep soul level. For a man without this nugget of wisdom, a wife's complaints or venting are usually his cue to run, find a project to work on, or suddenly become enthralled in the latest educational series on the Discovery channel. It would seem to most men that talking about these issues will not help, that their wives are simply being too negative and are making a big deal over something small. Some men are especially sensitive to negativity and believe that all their wife is doing is complaining about something that will never change, thus feeling frustrated and hopeless about her need to rant to him daily. But wives are looking for validation of our feelings, a support or reassurance that our husbands will stand by us through it all, that we are truly ok, and that we are not totally "losing it" as our emotions would be trying to convince us of in that moment.

Here are few (comical, yet fairly accurate) examples of how a man can "break" the code of reading his wife's emotions and suggestions for improving communication with his wife.

Words women use and what they **really** mean:
1. "Fine": This is the word women use to end an argument when they are right and you need to walk away.
2. "Five Minutes": If she is getting dressed, this means a half an hour. "Five minutes" is only five minutes if you have just been given five more minutes to watch the game before helping around the house.
3. "Nothing": This is the calm before the storm. This means something is wrong, and you should be on your toes. She is still getting ready to tell you what is bothering her. Arguments

that begin with "Nothing" usually end in "Fine."

4. "Go Ahead": This is a dare, not permission. Don't do it!

5. *Loud Sigh*: This is actually not a word, but it is a nonverbal statement often misunderstood by men. A loud sigh means she thinks you are an idiot and wonders why she is wasting her time trying to get you to understand how she feels or why she is upset. "You just don't **get** it," would be her thought to go along with her loud sigh.

6. "That's Okay": This is one of the most dangerous statements a woman can make to a man. That's okay means she is contemplating how many compliments, errands, flowers, and babysitting hours it will take to truly forgive you.

7. "Whatever": Is a woman's way of saying, "Go to H—"

8. "Don't worry about it, I got it": Gentlemen, you are in trouble now. This statement means that a woman has told a man to do something several times but is now doing it herself. This will later result in a man asking, "What's wrong?" For the woman's response, refer to number 3.

For a husband to be an excellent "code reader," it will require him to ask God to show him how to view his wife through the eyes of Christ. This means that through the logical, problem-solving eyes of a husband, it is irrational and ineffective to simply talk about feelings and not try to change the situation, the circumstances, or how one thinks. You can just throw out this kind of thinking, husbands; that is coming from your brain, not hers! Putting effort into accepting the fact that your wife is hardwired to express her thoughts and feelings differently than you, will help you be in a healthier place to start to listen and understand her from **her** point of view. This concept is truly the kind of care and validation most wives are so desperate to receive from their husbands.

Trying to have effective communication and a strong emotional connection with your wife will be impossible unless you have some spiritual wisdom to apply to these situations. Seeing your wife through God's eyes is seeing who God created her to be for His purpose and not seeing her as crazy or broken. I believe God will reveal to you that your wife is an amazing and wondrous creature, unique in how she loves, and that she nurtures and has compassion for others in ways that amaze you and greatly affect the world around her. In fact, your wife has traits and qualities that you will never quite understand because, as a man, you are not created to feel as deeply as she feels (it would be ineffective in times you need to be in your warrior-mode), and you will not think a bajillion thoughts at once, because your brain tends to compartmentalize. With this kind of insight and understanding about our differences, won't it be easier to tolerate her emotions and even offer comfort and forgiveness to your wife when her emotions are out of control or when she acts disrespectfully to you? When you develop your skill to "interpret" your wife's code words and female language, you will cultivate better communication and a stronger emotional connection and gain another skill as a Godly husband to keep in your "superhero tool belt" and truly become the spiritual leader in your relationship. You will experience a blessed family and feel the overall momentum in your life when you are fulfilling this husband role as God designed it.

> "Likewise husbands, live with your wives in an understanding way, showing honor to the woman as the weaker vessel, since they are heirs with you of the grace of life, so that your prayers may not be hindered."
> —I Peter 3:7

Review

- Learning your wife's language and how she uniquely expresses her emotions will help her feel close to you and you will have less conflict in your marriage.
- Your wife is not broken and will express her emotions in ways that seem foreign to men, but pursuing her and making an effort to understand her will make you a super husband.
- Ask God to see your wife through His eyes to supernaturally gain wisdom and appreciation for how she expresses herself and how you as a husband can be an expert in her individual language.

* * *

Heavenly Father,

I ask for your wisdom and insight in how I communicate and understand my wife. Help me in a supernatural way to be kind and comforting in times that I do not understand her. Give me direction and prompting in my Spirit that will direct me in conversations, urge me in times I need to pursue her, and quiet me in times I need to only offer comfort and not advance in my own agenda. I do not speak "wife code," but You do, Lord. Give me the wisdom and talent I need to be a skilled and loving husband, to understand and honor my wife in a way that would bless her and please You. Allow me to fulfill the role you have called me to, so that our prayers may be honored and answered by You.

In the name of Jesus, I pray.

Amen.

7

Mind Your OWN Backyard

"Let love be genuine. Abhor what is evil; hold fast to what is good. Love one another with brotherly affection. Outdo one another in showing honor."
—Romans 12:9–10

The focus of this chapter, and the key to having a healthy, thriving marriage, is that each of you care more about how you are honoring your spouse and God **more** than you care about how well your spouse is caring for or loving you. As Scripture says, how will you "outdo" one another by showing the love and grace of God to one another in the marital relationship?

"Mind your own backyard" is a counseling term we use that refers to focusing on improving yourself and not being so concerned about how others act, especially if that "other" is your spouse. It is very easy after a few years of marriage to have unresolved conflict and unforgiveness; that's when spouses begin to start "the List." The List might consist of: "She never appreciates anything I do for her. I clean the garage, I help with the kids, and I go to work every day, don't I?" The List is how we think of all the ways **we are great** and try to express love and serve our spouse, but feel like they fail to recognize or appreciate us. "He always takes me for granted. I feel like his mother, the maid, and a slave to the children. He never notices or appreciates how hard I work!"

If you are saying, "I don't really have a list" (which I doubt if you have been married for more than a week), remember the last time the two of you disagreed or had conflict, just for a second, did you think, "This isn't **my fault**! He/She is wrong, is not listening, or is being unreasonable!" Here is a bad recipe for the ongoing "list of hidden resentments" to develop:

- a difference in our thinking due to being man or woman
- inborn wirings/temperaments
- a poor childhood
- ongoing hurts and wounds
- Satan's lies in our head
- distance and disconnectedness between husband and wife

Good thing God has the **perfect recipe** for marriage: The two most important areas of marriage to focus on are . . . ready for it . . . sex and money? . . . Nope! Quality time with our spouse and communication? Wrong again! Parenting and getting our emotional needs met? No way! The two most important areas of marriage to focus on are our own spiritual walk with God and how we can have a deeper desire to serve our spouse. Hmmmm . . . think, chew, swallow . . . yes, swallow again; it's a tough one to process, isn't it?

But what about my needs? What about how he/she has treated me? Yes, those things are important too . . . but without doing some self-reflection and concentrating on the here and now, your marriage will never be successful. And, honestly, there is no true joy or contentment in getting our wants and needs met constantly; eventually we will just want and need more. It is an endless cycle and dissatisfying to say the least.

Being self-focused does **not** mean spending time thinking about your needs. It means thinking about the ways you could be a better spouse to your husband or wife. Even in the midst of what you believe might be them taking you for granted or feeling offended, the best way out of your misery and back into a "rewarding" relationship cycle is to **serve them**. I know you are probably thinking, "Are you serious? You don't know my situation. You don't know how long I have gone without my needs being met. I can't remember the last time my spouse served me. I don't believe my spouse will ever return the favor!" Perhaps you have even closed the book and thrown it in the trash by now . . . but if not, read on brave soldier.

If you attended Sunday school or vacation Bible school as a child, you might remember that familiar saying children are taught to ask themselves in difficult life situations: "What Would Jesus Do?" I used to have a rubber bracelet with this phrase on it: WWJD. Studying the New Testament and the use of parables told by Christ Himself, we can observe two main themes in His teachings: 1. Forgiveness. 2. Serving others.

As Christians, we are inspired to be Christ-like, so it is probably safe to say that forgiveness and serving are good advice for our marriage. After conflict or a hurtful time, instead of continuing to think about the ways in which you have been wronged and the lack of emotional comfort or respect-based care your spouse gave you, choose to focus first on forgiveness. "But he/she doesn't deserve it," you might say. Yes, but we did not **deserve** the ultimate sacrifice of Christ's death on the cross for our life either. He did it because He loved us! It was a gift from God; it costs us nothing and it is beyond our ability to **earn it**. It is this kind of forgiveness we can have for our spouse. Remember that forgiveness is a gift that is passed on from God, through Jesus, to us. It will be the greatest gift you ever give, and it only becomes more fruitful the more you choose to pass it on to others (and yourself).

Almost without fail, conflict within our marriage does not end well because of our human weaknesses and our own desire to get our needs met, our pride of needing to be right, or wanting to prove a point. It might end with both parties walking away and deciding to accept no resolution, but also feeling there is no hope or end in sight for this cycle of conflict. The couple becomes discouraged and might decide to accept that they will always disagree. Conflict without resolution always leads to hurts and wounds, many times more deeply for women because of our need for emotional resolution and because we have a sense of security and safety in being reassured that our husbands are not secretly mad or dissatisfied with us. A man can also have hurt feelings or unresolved anger due to feeling like his wife disrespects him over and over, which will affect his motivation to reconnect with her and even his general perception of how he sees his wife.

So the first step is to **not** make the list in our heads about how often or recent our spouse has offended us in the same way. It is not time to take inventory of all the great and wonderful things about ourselves in comparison to our spouse. It is not helpful to perseverate on how you would **never** treat them like they have just treated you. Now is the time to be self-reflective and use the character of Jesus as your comparison (just a word of warning; it might lead to a little conviction).

Step One: Whatever the spouse did to hurt you, state it aloud in this way, *"Father God, I forgive my spouse for _____ because I know it is pleasing to you and you sent Jesus to die for all sins, not just the ones I feel are justified. I choose to forgive my spouse and ask you to change my heart and view of him/her so that I see him/her through Your eyes. Return the love, care, and compassion to me that I once had for my spouse."* Notice how the prayer is basically handing the sin and situation over to God to handle? That's easy enough, right? You don't have to be the judge, you do not have to have feelings that match the verdict, all you need to do is release the offense from your heart, cast the angry or hurtful thought from your mind and give the **gift** of forgiveness as freely as it was given to you by our Father in Heaven.

That was one heck of a first step, and this will be easier at some times than others, but no matter how grave the hurt or offense, we are still called to forgive just as we have been forgiven. In counseling, I always remind people who struggle with forgiveness: Imagine if God "rated or weighted" your sin? What if He said, "Sorry, I can't forgive you anymore, you have made too many mistakes. You don't deserve to come to Heaven because you kept failing in the same ways"? What if God said He couldn't love you anymore because your words or actions have hurt Him too much? I pray that helps each one of us keep the failures of others, the hurts and distrustful actions of our spouse, into a new grace-filled perspective (remember, **grace** means undeserved favor and relentless forgiveness).

Step Two: Serve. Example: When my husband leaves his shoes right in front of the door over and over, as I trip on them, instead of cursing or kicking them across the room (now, who would do a thing like that? Ha!) I say, "I forgive him, Lord," and then I try to disregard the thought in my head of reminding him about it **the moment I see him**! Then I bend over, pick them up, and put them away. Oh, I hear you already ladies . . . "What? He can pick up his own shoes! I almost broke my neck, and he knows how much it bothers me to leave them **right** in front of the door. I am not his mother! When is the last time he put away my shoes, hung up my coat, or picked my underwear up off the floor?" But . . . what would Jesus do? (Hee-hee . . . it is wrong that it makes me laugh to imagine Jesus picking my husband's boxers up off the bathroom floor?) Every day, our marital relationship offers us the opportunity to offer grace and be Christ-like to our spouse through selflessly serving them.

Gentlemen, do not think this means I am telling your wives to go around picking up after you "in the name of Jesus." You have the same challenge as your wives, but it just looks a little different: when you get home from a long day at work and all you want to do is relax and watch your favorite show on TV or watch sports highlights on the internet, would you be willing to spend time with your wife instead? Spend quality time talking about her day and her feelings and **comfort her, making her feel like the most important thing in your life.** You are called to do this as husbands, even though the last words she spoke to you earlier that day were out of anger, complaint or disrespect. Not so easy, is it? Step one: forgive. Step two: serve.

You might be thinking, "How do I know how to serve my spouse in meaningful ways?" Ok, so that was probably not your next question. But, the answer of how to serve your spouse usually has to do with the "offense."

When I do parenting education or coaching classes, I instruct parents that the discipline given to children should fit the "crime" as much as possible. If the child swore, the consequence would be to have them write sentences that declare respect about their loved ones, and then they have to go twenty-four hours without being disrespectful verbally before any of their privileges are restored. If a child does not do a chore that was requested of them, the child will then be required to do their chore as well as the chore of another family member for as many days as they originally refused to do their chore. And so on.

In the area of marriage, if the offense was that the wife feels her husband does not listen to her and the conflict ended in her crying and him storming out of the home, the husband should try to plan a date night relatively close to the time the conflict occurred, then dedicate time on the date to intently listen to his wife's concerns and make her feel heard, not trying to correct her or become defensive about his actions, sending her the message she is the most important thing in his life and he will not rest until she believes that, as well as convincing her it was not his intent to hurt her with his actions. This takes a wise and strong man to complete this task. For the man to know and understand it is not about being weak or being "whipped," but that he is "man enough" to sacrifice his own righteousness to care for his wife's emotions and he is confident enough in who he is, to admit he might have had words or actions that hurt his wife, even if he felt he had done nothing wrong intentionally to hurt her. This really comes down to pride. What is more important, having a wife that is well-loved and a strong marriage, or being "right"?

What if the offense was something like a wife expressing her worry about money and then upsetting her husband in a way that makes him feel like all he does is work and she does not appreciate the fact he does his best to pay the bills? The wife could serve him by admitting she was being emotional and that she had anxiety about their money issues and giving him extra time alone to recoup and regenerate after work. Also, she can compliment him verbally or by a card/letter telling him how much she appreciates and respects him for working so hard and taking such good care of their family.

I believe both of these examples, if we are honest with ourselves, are very challenging. I am sure there are examples of conflicts or hurts and wounds that are flooding to your mind right now. You could be wondering how could I be serving my spouse or would I even really want to do so, during times of conflict? I would challenge you with this: Are you still hurt by past conflicts or times where you continue to lack resolution? Are there topics that are hot buttons between you and your spouse? Do you feel as close to your spouse as you would like? Do you have true satisfaction or fulfillment in your marriage? Then forgiveness and serving your spouse might be worth a try. It worked for Jesus.

Self-Reflection

So besides the behavioral or verbal list of what our spouse did or said wrong, we will also have the character or moral list: "He is so selfish, I bet God is really mad at him!" or "She is so kind to others, but if they only knew how she treated me!" The better approach, which is difficult to do in the moments following conflict but always more productive in having a healthy marriage, would sound like this: "What did **I** not do well, Lord? I ask you to convict me and help me change my ways so that I am pleasing to You and to my spouse. Please forgive me. Please help me have a servant's heart for my spouse." See what I just did there? I did not say, make an extensive list of your faults and make an action plan to try to change yourself. Simply ask God for guidance, ask for forgiveness from Him and ask Him to inspire you to have forgiveness in your heart for your spouse. Then focus on how you can fulfill your role in the marriage. If you are a husband, how can you be a better leader, pursue your wife and be the comforter of her feelings? If you are a wife, is it an issue of submission, being better at managing your own emotions, or about being a cheerleader and encourager to your husband? If we can reflect in prayer through God, He will always give us wisdom. Then we should turn to the Bible for further instruction. Focus on the example Christ set in how He served the people He met in His time of ministry, how He led his disciples through serving them or how He fulfilled His role in God's kingdom by dying on the cross for our sins. The best way to understand the heart and character of Christ is to read the gospels: Mark, Luke, John and Matthew. Meditate on the definitions of love in 1 Corinthians 13:4-7. Read the Proverbs, but do not try to think of how they apply to your spouse; instead, write down the ones you think you should memorize or internalize. This is about **you**! When you "mind your own backyard" the only things that can come out of this reflection are spiritual growth, a better marriage and additional intimacy with your Father God. How could that not be a good thing?

In addition, if you do give your spouse forgiveness and begin to serve them, I give you a money back guarantee that they will want to do the same for you. The only reason they would not, is if they do not believe your efforts are genuine. In that case, keep doing it until they are convinced. Besides, in all our efforts in life, our motivation needs to come from wanting to please God and fulfill our role in His kingdom and not because we are looking for the perfect reaction or gratitude from others as our reward. We will never be disappointed by God's love, favor and blessing in our life, but we will most certainly be disappointed by the failing, foolish reactions of the human beings in our lives, especially those "dirty traitors" we call our loved ones. (Just kidding, but you know that's how you think sometimes when you are mad at them and if you feel they have hurt you, ignored your kindness or your efforts. Especially if they reject your attempts at amends.) One of the most empty and joy-stealing misbeliefs we can have in life is that we will get the approval and appreciate **we think** we deserve from loved ones. That cannot be the reason we are motivated to serve others, or we will always lose the energy to do it. Trust God when He says your treasure on earth will only rust and rot away, but your reward in Heaven will be great and will last an eternity

(Paraphrased Matthew 6:19–20).

Abuse is NOT Ok.

I have given both men and women some pretty hard challenges so far in this book: to love and respect one another no matter the hurt of their spouse, to offer forgiveness, and submit to one another in ways that the rest of the world might say is weak or crazy. But let me be perfectly clear: abuse is not ok. The definition of abuse is lengthy, easily debatable, and can certainly be distorted. Physical abuse is the easiest to identify. Physically pushing/hitting one another or being physically hurt by a spouse is never allowed. Emotional abuse is harder to explain or identify, but it can be just as devastating as physical abuse. Name-calling, repeated put-downs, anger, blame, manipulation, making the spouse feel bad for who they are, intimidation, and isolation are a few behaviors of an emotionally abusive person. Hurts and wounds in a marriage can become so severe that a husband and wife can be equally abusive to each other. If you suspect you are being abused or are being abusive, seek help outside the marriage. Ask a trusted friend, a pastor or professional counselor for their opinion and perspective. Take time in prayer to reflect, and ask God if it is necessary to have a separation in the relationship for your physical or mental safety. Take this step with great thought and care.

Couples today split up too quickly, but there **are** situations in which staying in the marriage would be detrimental to the person, and God would not want you to take a risk with your life or well-being. Another situation that requires intervention is a spouse suffering from mental illness. This subject is more openly discussed today than in years previous, but at times, it can still be minimized and the marital relationship will very quickly become unhealthy and dysfunctional if someone is suffering from a mental health disorder. This might include depression, anxiety, OCD, ADHD, phobias, suicidality, self-injurious behaviors, eating disorders, bipolar disorder, personality disorders, or schizophrenia. If you are going to have a good marriage and stay individually healthy, early intervention is crucial. Speak to your doctor, seek counseling, and seek healing from Jesus. And, lastly, if there is drug or alcohol abuse/dependence or any addictive behaviors (gambling, pornography, spending, hoarding), the marriage will never improve unless the addict is in recovery. There are a lot of great recovery programs. Many are located within your local church community. It is not healthy, and it will eventually lead to problems within the marriage if you think **you** can handle your spouse or if the problem is simply ignored **you** will somehow manage. In all of these areas, it is most important to seek professional help. Problems within the marriage can become diluted, perverted and confusing at times, because you are too close to the issues; asking people you trust and probably ones that have professional training is always a good place to start.

Separation vs. Divorce

As Christians that have committed to a covenant love, we are challenged to ensure we have done everything we could to make our marriage work and have behaviors pleasing to God. This will ensure you are in a position to be healthy and spiritually blessed no matter what the outcome of your marital situation. If your spouse is abusive or an addict, a time of separation and working on yourselves individually can be an opportunity to improve and still retain the hope to reunify. If the person does not improve or follow through with promises for treatment or counseling, spend time in prayer and seek Godly advice before making the final decision to divorce. There are allowances for divorce, God will forgive you, and you **can** go on to have happy, healthy future relationships, but you must seek confirmation and have peace that your behaviors were pleasing to God first and that your spouse had the opportunity to change and fight for the marriage.

If your spouse is not a believer and you are, and they choose to leave the marriage or be unfaithful, the biblical advice is that the believer is to "let them go." But wait a good amount of time to allow God and the Holy Spirit to work on their heart before finalizing a divorce. I always recommend a year. A lot can change in a year. Press into God, and ask Him to heal old hurts and wounds. If the unbeliever is the one that wants the marriage to work, the believer should try to work it out. It is so important if you believe the marriage is not going to be saved to take time with God to heal before looking for or starting a new relationship. Once a spouse seeks a new relationship, emotional or physical, there is little hope for God to intervene and be able to resurrect the marriage.

If you have been separated and feel God is calling you both to try again, be sure to seek professional help for direction and encouragement. Old hurts and wounds can flare up and cause you to be overwhelmed or discouraged. Depending on how long you have been separated, coming back together might be tense or awkward and you will need a lot of prayer and support from others, but it is worth it. The couples we have counseled that have "survived" separation usually come back together with a renewed sense of commitment and hopefulness about how to have a better, more fulfilling marriage.

Review

- It is more important to focus on the ways you can change than how your spouse should change.
- Forgive your spouse, and forgive yourself.

- Serve like Christ served.
- Even in the midst of conflict and not getting your own needs met, you can serve your spouse and inspire a better relationship between you and your spouse.
- Abuse is not ok. Seek professional help.
- Marital separation and divorce is serious and has severe consequences, but it is allowable and forgiven by God.
- God is capable of saving any marriage if both spouses are willing.

* * *

Dear Father God,

Help me to be like Christ. Teach me how to forgive in difficult times and to be a servant, even when it is difficult. I want to understand the love and joy that comes with serving my spouse and being pleasing to You. I want to share the gift of forgiveness with others. I am so grateful you loved me enough to send Your one and only Son to die for my sins so that I am forgiven. I have no "right" to withhold that forgiveness from my spouse and I ask you to quickly remind me of this in times when my own hurt, anger, or righteousness get in the way of peace and closeness within my marriage. Alert me, Lord, to unhealthy behaviors within the marriage and bring healing and health to me, and my spouse in every area of our relationship. It is in You alone Lord that we trust with our marriage and it's future. In Jesus's name, we pray.

Amen.

8

Spiritual Healing for the Individual and as a Couple

"He himself bore our sins in His body on the tree, that we might die to sin and live to righteousness. By His wounds you have been healed."
—I Peter 2:24

Many marital problems are often a sign of a personal spiritual problem—a sin problem. Selfishness, pride, lack of compassion, unforgiveness, resentments, lust, anger . . . the list goes on and on. A person might argue, "But you don't know how unhappy I am! There is a reason I feel this way, and it has to do with my spouse, not my spirituality!" This chapter will address how each individual and the marriage can experience incredible healing, positive momentum, and joy by addressing matters of bondage, hurts, wounds, and other issues that have **affected** and damaged you as a person and as a couple.

After several years of biblical marriage counseling, my husband and I have experienced that **every couple**, without exception, has had individual spiritual problems that were affecting the marriage. Let's face it: unless you are Jesus and without sin, you will have "issues" and those issues need to be resolved or at least acknowledged in order to have true success in the marital relationship. That is why our cofacilitating model of counseling is so effective; we can spend sessions working separately, one-on-one, with the spouses of our respective sex. My husband can not only model for the other husband the strong-leadership role of a biblical husband, but also how to have spiritual deliverance and recovery from hurts, wounds, and strongholds that may be affecting the marriage and the overall success of that man's life. I will do the same with women and can offer biblical wisdom to the wife about ways in which she can become a Godly woman and learn to have spiritual and emotional freedom not just in her marriage, but in her whole life in general. She can learn to have spiritual contentment so that she no longer completely relies on her husband or kids for her fulfillment in life.

Most psychological and even faith-based counseling will spend a lot of time focused on your feelings, hurts, wounds, trauma in your past, and the condition of your current relationships. Your counseling experience is typically directed to analyze and adjust your current thinking to achieve a more hopeful attitude and outlook in life; these concepts and approaches are all important and helpful. But it has been revealed to me, by God, that incredible, lifelong healing and change can come from understanding who we are in His eyes, accepting strengths and weaknesses, and learning to look at ourselves and others in the world through spiritual lenses. Learning to look for healing and answers in God's person, character, and promises to us in His Word will bring you more peace and success in your life than you could ever have imagined. This is the kind of realization and healing that cannot be taken away by a bad circumstance, rejection from others, or a failure in your life.

When counseling individuals, I give them the ARNO temperament analysis assessment, and we go over it in the first or second session. I explain each of the areas and how their specific wirings (strengths and weaknesses) are a gift from God, but—due to our human, sinful nature—we seem to focus on the weaknesses. I also explain how we can begin to compensate for these weaknesses by applying spiritual wisdom and learning to submit these shortfalls and struggles to God—relying on His strength, not our own—to get us through failures and difficult times. Usually, this experience is very helpful for people. For some it can even change their self-esteem instantly, as they had always resented and rejected themselves for their weaknesses. Being aware of and accepting our strengths and weaknesses is only one small step in our overall spiritual walk. The most significant step—the one that will allow us to stay on God's path even when we feel weak, attacked, or alone—is feeling completely rooted in Christ.

Our Roots

Imagine a tree. This tree is fairly big and healthy to the human eye. But the actual strength of the tree depends on its roots below the earth. If a tree does not have deep, thriving roots, the first storm that comes along will knock it right over.

We are just like trees. If we are not firmly rooted in faith, we will be weak in times of attack by the Enemy, and we will be susceptible to believing negative things about ourselves or our lives. We will not be able to weather the storms of life very well without strong roots. The problem is that most people have their "roots" planted in what others think of them, or in how they view themselves, or whom their parents told them they were. "I am smart," "my parents loved me," "I am a good mother," etc. Others believe they know who they are and feel well rooted because of their accomplishments: "I am a good musician," "I have a lot of money," or "I have a master's degree."

But what happens when you are having a bad day and negativity creeps in? It is so easy for this to happen, and quickly we can believe such things as: "I am really not that smart," "I am not sure if my parents were ever proud of me," "I really do not feel like a good mother," or "Look at how naughty my children behave." It is easy to feel negative about our life accomplishments, because there will come a day (and more often than we would like) that we fail. Then how do we feel about ourselves? "I knew I wouldn't get that promotion at work," "I will never be able to afford a new car," "I just have horrible luck," or "There is always someone better than me." Being rooted in who we think we are based on our personality strengths, the approval of others, or our accomplishments will always leave us on unsteady ground, and then our "tree" is so much more vulnerable to the "storms" of life.

In order to have a tree that can withstand the most devastating of storms, we need to have three roots: God the Father; Jesus, our Redeemer and Savior; and the Holy Spirit that dwells within us.

The "God the Father" Root

Through this root we can experience unconditional love. In the earlier chapter entitled "Unconditional Love," we learned we couldn't accept this kind of deep, never-ending love with anyone other than our Heavenly Daddy. To believe and experience this kind of Fatherly love **can** and **will** heal all wounds left by our earthly parents, spouses, and any relationships. If you felt rejected by them, if they hurt or abused you in some way, or if you just never felt loved by them—whatever the scar left by your relationships, it can be healed by pursuing the deep and overwhelming love Father God has for you.

This root is also firmly planted within us if we understand God is our Creator. He is the Potter and we are the clay (Isaiah 64:8). Would he make something that was not beautiful and perfect in His eyes? I think not. I have had people argue, "Well God might not love me for who I am. I've made a lot of mistakes." But you see, that is where we can stray from the truth. The truth is that we are **all** flawed, and we all have a sinful nature. Our view of ourselves, others, and the world around us is continually tainted based on our hurts, wounds, assumptions, and the natural wirings of our temperament. The best we could ever imagine to see ourselves is to see ourselves through the eyes of the Creator, and only then could we truly appreciate the beautiful and wondrous piece of art God created us to be. He is perpetually in awe and in love with us, for He adores His own work.

Imagine if you could replace all the shortcomings, abuse, and trauma of your childhood and young adulthood with the picture of how much God loves you. None of us would ever suffer from "mommy" or "daddy" issues ever again. Besides, your parents were only human and sinners too. If we can forgive them for the ways they perhaps failed to love, protect, or nurture us and replant our need for love, security, and approval with the strength and unfailing love of our Heavenly Father, many wounds of our mind, soul, and emotions would be healed. And healing is the first step: the more we step into this faith and allow this "Father God root" to grow deep within us, the less we will be knocked down by the world and our relationships. Our internal confidence will be based on the fact that we are loved, significant, and capable and we will continue to grow in strength and perseverance for all of life's battles. Without a strong **grounding** in God's love for us as our Father and Creator, we will be easily tempted into feeling afraid, abandoned, unworthy, rejected, and worthless. So pursue conversations with God and gain an understanding of His love for you. As His creation, it is vitally important to be rooted in Him to be healthy—physically, spiritually, and emotionally. I would highly recommend the devotional *The Father's Love Letters* by Barry Adams.

The "Jesus" Root

The second root is the root of Jesus, our Savior. It represents how we are sinless and have no shame because of Jesus. We cannot out-sin His grace (Romans 5:20). No matter how we fail others or even let ourselves down, we can always rest in the righteousness of Christ. My dear friend and spiritual mentor, Marjorie Cole, once used this analogy: "We are all like diamonds. We are designed to **reflect the light of Jesus**, which is what makes us beautiful. A real diamond does the same; it does not go to sparkle school to **learn** to sparkle. It simply exists, by God's design, to reflect light. Thereby, it appears to be sparkling. But, if a diamond is covered in dust and is not able to reflect the light, it does not really sparkle; in fact, it could spend a lifetime hidden in a cave, covered in dirt and rock, and never have the chance to show its brilliance." We **need** Christ in our life to really sparkle; without **Him**, all we are left to focus on is our blemishes. For example, every teen girl I counsel complains about the same thing: they do not think they are pretty, smart enough, skinny enough; they do not like their hair, their butt, etc. But if we can focus on being a **diamond**, simply created to exist to reflect all of the brilliant qualities of Christ to the rest of the world, we cannot get that wrong! This is how we can embrace the root of Jesus within us.

Every time we feel offended by the world, put down, or rejected or have self-hate, we can turn to our Savior to redeem every failing quality within us. He died so that we could be righteous, but we have to believe it and apply His gift of forgiveness to our sins, or we will live miserably despite the fact he paid a price for us to live victoriously. When I think of it that way, it always helps to remind me not to waste such a precious gift. Besides, if I do not stay rooted in Jesus, the moment I begin to think I am happy with who I am or proud of an accomplishment, you can be sure something bad or negative will happen to take all those good, proud feelings away and leave what I thought was a beautiful, fruitful "tree" a dying withering mess, all over one mistake or failure. How do I stay rooted in Christ? Read the Bible. Understand the nature and character of Christ. Then accept that if you have received Jesus as your Savior and applied His gift of sacrifice for you (you have prayed the prayer from Chapter 5) then you already possess **every** one of those gifts and characteristics of Jesus in **you**. That automatically makes you amazingly awesome, forever, everyday, no matter your success or failure or how much others appreciate or approve of you. The amazing concept of receiving a gift such as the forgiveness through Christ is that you did nothing to deserve it and there is nothing you can do to make God take it away from you. You are forever changed when you accept Jesus as your Savior, and that is something to lean on. Reflect on that when you have times of rejection or failure. You are a diamond, and you were created to sparkle. Not because you tried really hard to do so, not because of your efforts or achievements, but because you were made pure, holy, and brilliant through the blood of Christ. An excellent resource to help you understand the overwhelming revelation of grace is Joseph Prince's *Unmerited Favor*.

The "Holy Spirit" Root

The last root is planted in the Holy Spirit. When you give your life to God and ask Christ to be your Savior, you have eternal life in Heaven. Another benefit is that you also receive the Holy Spirit—that is the Spirit of God that dwells within you, here on earth. It never leaves you, but you can choose to ignore Him or you can learn to **really** listen to Him and nurture your relationship with Him. I believe the Holy Spirit is the least studied of the Trinity and He is so vital in our life as Christians. We need to rely on this root of the Holy Spirit for God-given wisdom, direction, and guidance in our life. If we rely on our own human understanding of ourselves, others, and this world, we will always fall short and be disappointed. We will make poor decisions based on our sinful nature, desires, and temptations. We will have a great deal of stress and anxiety about making decisions or trying to make changes in our life without spiritual guidance. If we can learn how to tap into the power of the Holy Spirit, our decisions can become good ones, our lives will be more successful, we will have less fear, and every time we stray off the path, we will quickly return to the road God has for us, based on the gentle urging of the Holy Spirit. Our efforts in work, marriage, and life in general will have momentum, we will have motivation and self-control, and we will be able to make changes in our lives in an instant with this supernatural power and wisdom.

I have learned an easy way to determine whether I am staying tapped into the Spirit: stress, anger, distress, and confusion are "dashboard indicators" that my Spirit is on "empty." God gives us the Holy Spirit as a direct line of communication with Him. But we do need to work on learning to use this gift. Just like a new piece of technology, there is a learning curve. Time needs to be spent learning the application of this supernatural tool, and then, through trial and error, we can become Holy Spirit experts and confident in our ability to use Him to guide us in the ways that are pleasing to God. Time in prayer, worship, and reading the Word renew our Spirit. Then we can enjoy all the fruits of the Spirit

(Galatians 5:22–23), which will trump any stress or problem the world can dish out. To assist in this effort I would recommend the book by John Bevere simply entitled, *The Holy Spirit*, which offers a study guide component.

This discernment works with negative feelings as well. If we have uneasiness or upset feelings, we need to examine whether or not we are trying to go against our Spirit. If there are thoughts or behaviors that would not be pleasing to God, we are going to feel Him poking us from the inside out through our Spirit. Do not worry. God is gentle, understanding, and relentless in teaching us His ways. Our biggest responsibility is to simply be obedient and rely on the Guide He gave us through the gift of the Holy Spirit.

The Invincible Tree

So let's review how strong your "tree" is **now:**

1. You are firmly rooted in unconditional love and cannot **ever** be rejected from the family of God. This love will ensure all your life wounds past, current and future will heal. And you are **never, ever** alone. God always has you in the palm of His hand.

2. You have the spectacular beauty of a diamond that could blind the world with its brilliance if you allow the light of Jesus to reflect through you! This will ensure you will **never** be seen as a failure, inadequate, shameful, or not good enough. You are all God created you to be, with an unending, lifetime stamp-of-approval that can never tarnish.

3. Lastly, you have the ability to make good decisions, make dynamic changes in your life, grow in wisdom and confidence, and have tremendous supernatural abilities and transformations; all that come through the power and fruits of the Holy Spirit.

This tree isn't going anywhere! You are now unoffendable and indestructible and have continual life through the Living Waters: God, Jesus, and the Holy Spirit.

> "Blessed is the man who trusts in the Lord, whose trust is the Lord. He is like a tree planted by water, that sends out its roots by the stream, and does not fear when heat comes, for its leaves remain green, and is not anxious in the year of drought for it does not cease to bear fruit."
> —Jeremiah 17:7–8

Why did I spend so much time going into all this "rooted stuff" and a person's sense of self when this is supposed to be a book about marriage and relationships? Because, without this firm foundation in our identity and worth in Christ, we will always struggle in life, especially in our relationships. On the contrary, as long as we know who God created us to be and have the faith and skills to apply our supernatural rooting . . . we are unstoppable, relationship machines!

Your Spiritual Walk As a Couple

Common marriage statistics are as follows: Divorce rate of non–Christian believers is 50 percent. Divorce rate of couples that would say they are "Christian" is 50 percent. Divorce rate of Christians who read the Bible, go to church, and pray together, as a couple, is less than 5 percent. The truth is, having God at the center of your marriage, the One you **both** turn to in difficult times, is the only answer to having a lifelong, fulfilling marriage. Husbands, it is your role to be the spiritual leader. That means making reading the Bible, prayer, and going to church a priority for you, your wife, and your children. Your household will go where **you lead it**. Prayer is crucial in the physical and emotional health of both husband and wife. The power of prayer during difficult times in life will be the difference between a marriage crisis and the strengthening of your marriage exponentially. After every conflict, a couple should pray together to ensure they have both granted each other forgiveness. Then they should ask God to restore peace and closeness within their relationship. I would highly recommend *The Power of Prayer to Change Your Marriage* by Stormie Omartian.

An important area in a marriage that drastically improves by being Christ-centered is parenting. A husband and wife who are equally yoked in faith, are on the same page spiritually, and turn to the Bible for parenting wisdom will have very few arguments about child-rearing, and together they can become a parenting powerhouse! A wonderful, biblical parenting resource is Michelle Anthony's *Spiritual Parenting*. If this is an area of conflict within your marriage, I urge you and your spouse to seek resolution, support one another, and fall into the biblical roles God has called you to fulfill to inspire your children to have the most blessed and hopeful future possible.

Out of Reverence for Christ

Our purpose and motivation in marriage, parenting, and life in general **must always only** be for the glory of God. What does that really mean? The truth lies in Scripture. Over and over in the Bible, God gently reminds us that our works here on this earth are for His pleasure, the purpose of His Kingdom, and to fulfill His plan. Then we are called to give all the glory (credit, honor, and praise) to Him, for without Him we could not achieve any of it. Giving praise to Him helps remind us that our life is not **all** about us or what we want in life. True happiness comes in being grateful for our life, having spiritual and emotional freedom, and attaining our eternity in Heaven, which are all gifts from God. He truly does deserve the praise!

The truth is, our efforts, our attempts at success, and even our very existence are purposeless if it not for our relationship with God. You might ask, "Doesn't God care if we are happy. Don't I get credit for how hard I try?" The answer is: He is more concerned with your salvation (whether you spend eternity with Him) and the mission of bringing the Good News of the gospel to others than your "happiness."

This doesn't mean God doesn't want us to have the desires of our heart or that we won't have times when we are enjoying blessings in our life, but it cannot be our focus and definitely cannot be our expectation in order to be emotionally stable or have joy in our lives. God loves His children and will show them favor and give them blessings many times throughout their lifetime, but there will also be times where we will not get our needs or desires met, and then how will we react? We must be grateful for these difficult times too. Most of the things we selfishly seek to satisfy our human needs and desires will inevitably lead to emptiness. Think about it: New clothes get old, shrink (especially in my washing machine), or lose their fashion. A new car gets scratched, dirty, dented, and stops running eventually. Even a fancy vacation will be over in seven to ten days. Then what?

> *"Do not lay up for yourselves treasures on earth, where moth and rust destroy and where thieves break in and steal, but lay up for yourselves treasures in heaven, where neither moth nor rust destroys and where thieves do not break in and steal. For where your treasure is, there your heart will be also.*
> *—Matthew 6:19–21*

Does that mean we should not enjoy a new outfit, a nice car, or a vacation? Of course not. But our hearts cannot be too tightly bound to these earthly things. It is truly the secret to having joy and being content in life and within your marriage.

> "Set your mind and affections on things above, not on things that are on earth."
> —Colossians 3:2

What would our marriage look like if we did things out of reverence for Christ? Well, let's start with the little things: It might be a wife acting motivated to encourage her husband with a work issue. Even though his response is negative or defeating, she continues to pray for him, lift him up, and be positive with him . . . out of reverence for Christ. It is defeating and frankly impossible to encourage our spouse when they give us no positive response. A common complaint I hear in counseling is, "Well I tried to be positive, but he/she was so negative, I just gave up." Does Jesus give up on you? Without having a Christ-like mindset, we will give up on our efforts to be loving or respectful because we are getting no accolades, appreciation, or validation that it is "working." When our motivation for being encouraging to our spouse is that we know it would be pleasing to God and we are being a blessing to someone else, then we will be fulfilling our role in God's plan and purpose for our life. There are also emotional and spiritual blessings that come from this kind of behavior. I can love, respect, and serve my spouse for **those reasons**. But if your reason or motivation for being sacrificial to your spouse is because of what you hope to get in return or to see some change in your spouse, then you will surely be disappointed and quickly give up on trying to make the marriage better.

An example for what a man will do to serve his wife out of reverence for Christ might be this: The wife is upset, emotional and seems to take it out on him, and he is feeling very disrespected by her. But he will make a choice to respond with love and emotional care for her. At this point in the book, we have established that men do not do well with being disrespected, especially by their wives. We have equally acknowledged that when a woman is hurt, wounded, or feeling overwhelmed, she may act disrespectfully without knowing it due to her emotional state of mind. So by instinct and in your weaknesses, gentlemen, it would be easy to ignore her, avoid her, or snap back due to feeling disrespected. But, husbands, you can act out of pure obedience to God and still listen to her, comfort her (even when her "claws and a sharp tongue" are coming at you), and embrace her to ensure she understands you will be there for her, no matter what. Tough, huh, guys? But you can do it! You have the strength of Christ within you. And when we really search our hearts for how much God loves us and has sacrificed for us, this is one small act of grace we can offer the person we are supposed to love **more than anyone else**. This is also another great example of how a man is called to love his wife like Christ loves the church. For a husband to sacrifice that which is so important to him, his respect, in order to meet the needs of his wife is one of the best Christ-like behaviors he can have. Christ gave up his life for you; can you hang your "right" to be respected on the cross for the health and benefit of your marriage?

Here is one more example: The marriage is at a breaking point, and you think it is destined for divorce for sure. You cannot imagine loving your spouse ever again after all the hurt that is between you. You feel beyond discouraged, and you are hopeless. You could leave the marriage and try to seek happiness with someone else, but is that really God's intention for your marriage?

God would call you to be an example of Christ's love; you need to sacrifice your desires and human needs to serve your spouse, even if they reject you. There is no way we could have this kind of strength without the Holy Spirit and our Savior, Jesus, within us for strength. That is why so many marriages end in divorce. Not that there wasn't any hope for their marriage, but because the couple failed to tap into the resurrecting and supernatural power of our Lord Jesus Christ, because through Him **all things** are possible and we will not run out of ambition to keep fighting for our marriage! A spouse that can serve, love, and support the other spouse, even in the midst of the other spouse trying to leave them or stab them in the back, will be protected and blessed by God. The blessings might be that their dissatisfied spouse will see their intentions and unfailing love right away and reconnect. Sometimes, the blessings might come later in another area of their life, but either way, if that spouse's actions and heart are pleasing to God they will be creating blessings and favor in their life beyond human reason or rationale. God rewards you for your efforts—maybe not how you were expecting—so be vigilant for His gifts and always, always be grateful.

Husbands, if your wife says she wants to leave you and does not love you anymore, it is most likely caused by years of hurt and damage or due to a lack of emotional care or connection with her. This is the time to ask her to tell you about the ways you have hurt her, neglected her, or how you have fallen short of her expectations. Then you can seek to ask for her forgiveness. No "I'm sorrys." "I'm sorry" is a one-sided statement, but asking for forgiveness requires a response and a **granting** of the gift of forgiveness, which will cause her heart to change too. Make an effort to truly understand how you made her feel (do not get defensive), ask her to forgive you, and be ok with her need for more time to grieve or decide whether she is ready to forgive you; you are strong and courageous men, and you can do it. Then offer her love, comfort, and reassurance of your efforts to emotionally care for her until the end of time. Do this all despite her reaction. She might reject you, or she might be confused and need time to think. If she has gotten to the point of wanting a divorce, she will definitely need time to build up the courage to trust you enough to want to try again. Through all of her emotional turmoil, you will need to be strong and be confident that you are doing the right thing based on your role in the marriage and God's approval of you. Your greatest challenge will be to resist defending your actions, accusing her back of her failures, or getting too focused on how your performance in the marriage is never good enough for her. Be strong and in tune with God's voice and allow her to express her hurt, and then respond in heartfelt earnest that you want to do better and be the husband she needs you to be. Truly you will be walking out a Christ-like example by fulfilling this role in your marriage.

A "big one" for women, in order to be acting out of reverence for Christ, would be if her husband does not show he cares about her and he is not motivated to meet her needs. Either he is not a Jesus-follower and is not motivated by the Holy Spirit, or he has given up, hopeless after years of feeling he is inadequate or incapable of meeting his wife's needs. There are times a man will be the one who does not feel loved or wants to leave the marriage. Women have this significant role in the marriage: we are called to be respectful and courageous by controlling our thoughts and emotions and to resist trying to control him or the situation. We, too, can rely on God to get us through, and we can be loving and respectful and fulfill our role in the marriage despite the decision our husband makes. If a wife can continue to show her husband respect and yet not act overly reliant on her husband and rely on God in difficult times, her good intentions will be evident to the husband and **inspire** him to continue to work on the marriage too.

The most beautiful thing about acting out of reverence for Christ and relying on God in difficult times is that we will inevitably grow spiritually stronger through this experience and continue to build our faith that God can get us through anything in life, no matter what. Even our marriage problems. God loves you and wants you to understand submission because it offers peace, security, and rest. When you feel like you can no longer fight for your marriage or please your spouse, rely on Him and He **will** resurrect your life, one way or another.

Review

- Your spiritual journey and overall spiritual health affect your marriage.
- Do not rely on your spouse to fulfill your spiritual needs.
- Strengthen your roots to be steadfast in all of life's storms.
- We inherit characteristics and attributes from God the Father, Jesus, and the Holy Spirit.
- Your spiritual walk as a couple drastically affects the success and fulfillment in the marriage.
- Through faith, we receive supernatural energy and motivation to forgive and serve our spouse.
- Acting out of reverence for Christ in how we serve and forgive our spouse is part of our spiritual growth.

✳ ✳ ✳

Dear Heavenly Father,

I believe I am alone, anxious, and stressed and lack grounding in my life without being rooted in You. I ask you to reveal to me in deeper and more meaningful ways how I can stay rooted in You and adapt all the attributes of the Holy Trinity. Help me to see myself and my spouse through Your eyes. Reveal to me true grace and righteousness that was not earned, but a gift to me from the sacrificial gift of Your Son, Jesus, who died on the cross for my sins. Help remind me of this great and loving sacrifice in times when I struggle to forgive myself and others. Forgiveness, holiness, purpose, and my individual design are all gifts freely given to me by You; therefore, I can and will give love and forgiveness and be motivated to fulfill my role within my marriage out of reverence and gratitude to Christ. Use the Holy Spirit to guide me and prompt me when I forget these important gifts and forget by trying to do life on my own without You. I stand in agreement today that I am well rooted in You and will continue to grow in faith and servanthood because You are my Sustaining Water.

In Your precious and holy name, I pray,

Amen.

9

How to Stop the Attack Cycle

"Have nothing to do with foolish, ignorant controversies; you know that they breed quarrels. And the Lord's servant must not be quarrelsome but kind to everyone, able to teach, patiently enduring evil, correcting his opponents with gentleness."
—2 Timothy 2:23–24

This chapter will address the reasons couples tend to fall out of healthy cycles of mutual respect and love and a strong emotional connection with each other. Having insight into the common pitfalls in marriage will enable you as a couple to be more proactive and intervene with healthy strategies to prevent major disconnection.

Here are five main reasons husbands and wives will feel attacked by each other and lack conflict resolution in the marriage:

1. There are unforgiven/unresolved hurts and wounds that cause the individual to have an assumption or predisposed reaction to their spouse based on past conflict.

2. One or both of the individuals have not been honest about their feelings and there has been unresolved grief or internalized anger, and now they are reacting harsher than the actual situation calls for.

3. The individual has gone a long time not getting their emotional/temperament needs met.

4. Past issues such as family of origin, past romantic relationships, or other friendships have wounded the person and left them feeling vulnerable or sensitive to certain relationship issues.

5. We make our spouse "the problem" instead of focusing on the spouse's **valid** needs that are not like our own, or we do not take into consideration the spiritual warfare affecting the situation.

I am sure there are many more, but these are the most common ones my husband and I address in our counseling sessions with couples. Resolving conflict and healing the feelings of being attacked in the marital relationship can determine the emotional bond and closeness of the couple, which is so crucial to having a happy and functioning marriage. If these issues are not addressed and properly healed, the relationship will start to deteriorate and sometimes, if left long enough in this withering stage, can feel like it is hopeless and beyond repair.

1. There are old hurts and wounds in the marital relationship that cause the individual to have an assumption or predisposed reaction to the other spouse based on past conflict.

I chose to list this one first because it seems to be the most common in the couples we have counseled. Inevitably, in a marriage there will be conflicts and things said out of anger, frustrations, grief, or haste. An example: A husband has often felt disrespected by his wife while first entering his home after coming home from work; therefore, he has a predisposition to feel like she is always in a bad mood and ready to "attack" or nag as soon as he walks in the door. Then one day, the wife goes to her husband for emotional comfort about a difficult day with the children, and the husband walks away and tells her he "can't take it anymore" and that she is negative and complains all the time. The wife is hurt and angry that her husband would not only make her feel bad about coming to him for support, but also feels like her character or who she is as a person is being attacked by him. She would most likely become defensive and perhaps even criticize the husband for his weaknesses or lack of ability to comfort her. He would then see this as **more** proof of how negative she is and how she is always against him. Now this conflict has created more hurt and will be more difficult to resolve. I am sure many couples can relate and one can certainly see how easily a conversation could get out of hand and become attacking.

Let's analyze what went wrong: First of all, do not feel bad or defensive if this describes you. This happens to all of us, and it is in our human nature to defend or attack during conflict situations. There is instinctual momentum that starts to occur when dealing with the male and female brains, temperament needs, and wounds of the soul that drastically affects the outcome of our conflicts. Because our feelings of love, the primal need to connect, and the desire for closeness in the relationship, conflict and hurts can cause both men and women to be more irrational and aggressive and fall to the lowest of our weaknesses, which will cause less-than-desirable behaviors to come out.

The first concept to understand is that the husband has not been honest with his wife about how often in the past he has felt disrespected by her complaining. Men do not usually talk about these things because they are emotional feelings, and a man will assume if he talks about it, things could just get worse or he might upset his wife and cause more conflict. On the contrary, this lack of openness and transparent honesty with his wife fosters built up frustrations and resentments inside of him. Men need to learn how to be more expressive and vulnerable when it comes to feelings. They need to be able to talk to their wives about how they feel in a way that a woman can understand without feeling defensive. Not only will this help with communication, but it will also do wonders for the emotional connection a man will have with his wife. As women we **love** to talk about feelings. There is also a helpful component of this for the husband. It allows him to have forgiveness for his wife and not allow harsh or resentful feelings to build up inside of him that would cause him to be less kind and compassionate towards his wife. This work is his to do **within himself**, with God's help, using Christ as his example.

We can acknowledge that the wife in this example just wants to be emotionally close to her husband and have her feelings understood and validated by her husband; she cannot wait for him to come home so she can vent about the stresses of her day to him, problem-solve with him, and seek comfort from him whom she relies on to be her emotional rock and anchor. To most men, emotions are a difficult thing to deal with and understand in women. Feelings can be intimidating and actually scary to many husbands. But because she is emotional, especially depending on her temperament, she will most likely express a lot of emotion outwardly and rather than appearing to need emotional care, the wife might look more like a forked-tongue cobra coming at him. The opposite of the outward expression of emotions is that some women will not say anything at all but then have hidden anger and resentment that becomes harder and harder for them to forgive. Our husbands might have no idea we feel this way, causing a great disconnect in our marriages.

I admit, I do not always appear to be June Cleaver to my husband either, standing with a tasty meatloaf and a warm smile waiting at the door for him when he gets home from work. (Although,

I do make a rocking meatloaf; it is the cheesy smile and string of pearls I haven't been able to pull off yet!) Because of past experiences, the husband is already expecting the conflict or negativity of his wife when he comes home from work and will be quick to react to **any** negative emotion his wife might express. The tricky part for wives is that we need to be **talented** enough to express our emotional, spiritual, or stress-related needs in a way that our husbands could receive it and not feel disrespected by us. Likely, a better approach would be waiting until he has had time to decompress from his day and then approach him with a request for a "listening ear." Be considerate of his energy or tiredness level, and remind him you just need to vent and do not expect him to solve all your problems or feel it is his fault that you feel the way you do.

A challenge to the husband: most men work very hard at their jobs and usually when they come home, they are looking for it to be a sanctuary, a time to rest and restore. But please understand, husbands, there are a wife and probably children who will be craving your **attention**, **affection**, and **affirmation**. It is a lot to ask of you, to sacrifice your much-needed time to rest and then to also be resilient in times of feeling attacked, but God put the strength and courage in you to do it. You will need to be prayerful about it—perhaps you decide to include it in your morning prayers or even on your drive home—but prepare yourself mentally and spiritually to be able to lead your household emotionally when you walk through the door. Protect your mind and heart from past conflict or fear of future conflict and approach your wife with the assignment (from God) to love and emotionally care for her. If you can successfully comfort what might look like a "vicious serpent" (a wife that is upset and venting), she will quickly turn into a squishy teddy bear, ready to submit and to enjoy a great big hug from you—her warrior, her protector, and her hero. Husbands, part of your prayer might be casting out lies in your head such as: your wife is offensive, negative, an emotional mess, stressful to you, attacking you, etc. Shut down your analytical brain when it tries to rationalize what she is doing wrong, how you try to serve her and your family and now she is ungrateful, or the ways she has offended you in the past. Forgive her, stay in the present and approach her and your family with a renewed sense of joy and willingness to serve them that can only come from the Spirit within you, not of your own ability or ambition. Cast a vision of who she is in the eyes of Christ, and see her **that way** when she comes to you with her grievances, even if they are specifically about you. Listen to her and comfort her in a Christ-like way and watch her anger, defensiveness, and grief melt away. If you can do this, not only will you achieve sainthood, but your emotional connectedness as a couple will soar. This does not mean the two of you will never have conflict, but it will certainly be less frequent and less intense and your marriage will be strengthened in the process.

2. One or both of the individuals has not been honest about their feelings. There has been unresolved grief or internalized anger and now they are reacting harsher than the actual situation calls for.

Example: The husband is watching TV and the wife wants to tell him something important about her feelings. She can see he is distracted and is torn as to whether she should even try, but her need to feel heard and the desire to connect with her husband drives her to start talking. Being the emotionally intuitive creature that she is, she quickly senses he is **not** hearing her or really paying attention. The thoughts in her head sound a little like this, "Why does he pay attention so closely to this TV where people are falling down off their skateboards, working on a car, or building an outhouse in Alaska? I am his wife; doesn't he know what I do for him and how much I sacrifice? He cannot even pay attention to me and pretend like he cares about what I have to say! He always pays attention when his buddies call or when it has to do with business. Then he can be attentive for hours. Look at him oh-so-intently watching this TV program. I wish he would look at me in like that. He can recall the score of a game from two weeks ago and he will be able to recall the step-by-step instructions on how to make coat hangers from watching *How It's Made*, but he has no idea what I just said. Argh!"

Women will have an internal monologue like this when they have either not expressed their true feelings to their husband or they have not received the emotional validation to resolve their feelings in the past when they did try to express them. With this lengthy assumption in the wife's mind already affecting her emotions, approaching her husband for a conversation when she knows he is distracted will turn into a full-blown fight. Another option is that the wife will not attempt to connect with her spouse and just resent the heck out of him on the inside. The poor guy has no idea she feels this way and he is probably just trying to relax after a long day. The skill that wives need in this situation is how to approach their spouse. She will need to refrain from expressing her emotions in an offensive or disrespectful way. Even though she feels he has ignored her or neglected her in the past, not saying anything is not helpful to us in getting our needs met. Silence creates distance in the relationship along with internalized anger, and it is unfair to men who do not have the emotional radar or crystal ball to be able to read their wife's mind. It is so important for both husbands and wives to be honest about their feelings, even if they are afraid it will cause more conflict. Resolution to hurts, wounds, and past offenses are the key to less frequent conflict and less explosive emotions within each conflict. This will take strength, courage, vulnerability, and resilience, because it does not always turn out the way we would like, which is why most people stop talking about how they feel and storing up the hurt on the inside in the first place. Once again, I would instruct you to go against your natural instinct to self-preserve or retreat; you can do it! Seek God's wisdom and be prayerful about your words and attempts to resolve the internalized feelings. Both men and women will need to acknowledge how they hurt one another (even if that was not their intention) and forgive one another for these feelings to truly go away for good. If it does not go well on the first attempt, pray about it and try again. Do not give up on achieving healing and resolution in your marriage; it is the key to a long-lasting love and connection with your spouse.

3. The individual's emotional/temperament needs have not been met for some time.

In the previous two examples, I pointed out that a husband might go a long time without feeling respected by his wife or a wife might feel unloved and uncared for by her husband. The complicated aspect of fulfilling the needs of your spouse is that their needs are usually quite different than your own. First, due to the fact men and women have different needs and desires and second, because of individual temperament needs. Feeling competent to meet **all** of your spouse's needs in order to prevent conflict or negative emotions between each other can leave a couple feeling exhausted and hopeless. Well, there is good news. Having a good marriage, having less conflict, and stopping the attack cycle do not require that you perfectly meet all of your spouse's needs. What is necessary is that in the midst of conflict and to prevent another attack cycle from occurring it is important for the individuals to acknowledge that the lack of these needs being met might be the reason that our spouse is offensive or defensive. This insight should instigate sympathy, compassion, and a willingness to acknowledge that for the other person. Validate that there is a reason they are reacting so harshly, and ask for forgiveness for the part you might have had in depleting those needs, and with love and sincerity ask them how you could play a part in lifting them up again. Notice how I said "a part." A spouse can only do so much to give love and reassurance to the other spouse. Sometimes the emotional or temperament need is something the individual needs to seek from God through prayer, or something they need to work through with a professional counselor. But if we, as loving and respecting couples, make an effort when we see our spouse upset and struggling during conflict to give them grace and understanding rather than join in on the attack cycle, we will see our spouse and the marriage flourish.

4. Past issues such as family of origin, past romantic relationships, or other friendships that wounded the person have left them feeling vulnerable or sensitive to certain relationship issues.

I believe this can be a very difficult area to address, heal from, and overcome without outside professional help. Perhaps individual counseling is necessary to address these issues, maybe couples counseling, mentoring from a mature Christian couple, and most definitely through spiritual healing from Christ. This topic can cause horrible marital conflict and areas of personal weaknesses where attack cycles can set in, especially if the individual has had an unhealthy childhood or abusive past relationships or if they have experienced any kind of trauma. Let's face it: this describes most of us. Not many people escape childhood, young adult dating, or the beginnings of a new marriage without some kind of emotional damage. Especially, for those of you in a second marriage, beware of making your current spouse pay for your ex-spouse's sins.

One of the ways our past can hurt our current relationship is in the area of "repeated offense." It is inevitable that each spouse will begin to feel that the other person repeatedly hurts them in certain ways; this is an indicator of a temperament weakness. So isn't it logical that our family of origin and previous relationships would have hit a chord with those same weakness previously? Rejection, self-esteem, neglect, criticism: whatever your trigger or area of hurt might be, you can be guaranteed that people in your life will make you feel wounded in those same areas over and over. In healthy relationships, while dating/courting the couple will have discussed possible areas of weakness and pitfalls that were apparent in other relationships. This will not ensure these areas will never be a problem again, but it will give the spouse insight in times the other spouse might struggle. Then they can be caring and encouraging of one another. Unfortunately, due to heated feelings and cycles of unresolved conflict, this valuable information might be used against a spouse as a weapon of attack during conflict.

It is our responsibility as loving spouses and followers of Christ to withhold our assumptions or emotional reactions by using our spouse's past hurts or weaknesses against them. A common fault of conflict that couples will complain about might sound like, "I tried to be honest and share my hurts with him, but he just threw it in my face later." This can start to destroy the trust and vulnerability that is so important in marriage. The couple can become fearful that past issues will continue to hurt them; therefore, they will try to protect themselves from being hurt or attacked by their spouse, creating defensiveness and distance in the relationship. The truth is that we will never completely treat each other perfectly, and being forgiving and remembering our spouse probably has good intentions behind their less-than-perfect actions will help instigate compassion and forgiveness for them in times that we feel the "repeated offense." Then we need to give them grace for the fact that our intense hurt or negative reaction might be compounded by wounds not inflicted by our spouse or this particular conflict, but conflicts in the past by many different offenders and our spouse did not create all of those feelings in one circumstance or conflict.

5. We make our spouse "the problem" instead of focusing on the spouse's needs and taking into consideration the spiritual warfare that can affect the situation.

A natural instinct in humans is that when we feel attacked, we attack back. When our emotional needs are not met—when a man feels disrespected or when a woman feels unloved—whose fault could that be? Our spouse is to blame, right? One helpful result in conflict that will improve emotional closeness is if both individuals in the relationship focus on how to make the **other** spouse feel validated and not continue to blame or accuse each other for the reason or trigger of how the conflict began.

With a logical mind, we could analyze a conflict between husband and wife line by line. Or we could even video tape them and dissect each word and behavior to determine who started it and who is to blame. But is that really what will improve the marriage? Is it really going to bring about a stronger emotional and spiritual bond between the couple to point fingers or place blame? Will it actually result in never having conflict again if the blame is assigned to one spouse or another? Again, it is human nature to want justice, fairness, and to have our rights be acknowledged by the other person. But often in marriage, what is "right" or healthy is not about our "rights." If we can turn from our own selfish needs and desires to be right, heard, or validated and use Godly discipline to care more for our spouse than ourselves, we will see an amazingly strong marriage—a bond that cannot be destroyed—develop. In order to do this, we must not allow ourselves or Satan to convince us that our spouse is the problem. Perhaps the problem is miscommunication, or perhaps it is past unresolved grief/wounds. It might even be straight-out warfare from the Enemy trying to destroy your marriage and family by convincing you of lies about your spouse. Be aware the more you do for God's kingdom and the more your marriage can make a difference in the world, the more Satan will lie and deceive you to try to destroy your relationship with God and your spouse.

> "Be sober-minded; be watchful. Your adversary the devil prowls around like a roaring lion, seeking someone to devour."
> —1 Peter 5:8

It is so helpful when we acknowledge a great deal of the emotional and relationship problems we have in life are all part of **Satan's plan** to make us less effective for **God's plan** for our life. The answer is that we can pray for protection in the name of Jesus, put the blame where it belongs (evil spiritual forces), and turn to God and the Holy Spirit for wisdom and truth rather than listen to the lies of the Enemy. Our spouse is not the enemy that we need to attack; Satan is. The offenses and hurts caused by our spouse are forgivable, but Satan will try to stir them up inside of you, cause you great agony, and make you weary, eventually making you turn on your spouse. Armor up against these attacks and do so hand-in-hand with your spouse. Your battle is not against your husband/wife, but rather the evil of this world.

> *"Finally, be strong in the Lord and in the strength of his might. Put on the whole armor of God, that you may be able to stand against the schemes of the devil. For we do not wrestle against flesh and blood, but against the rulers, against the authorities, against the cosmic powers over this present darkness, against the spiritual forces of evil in the heavenly places. Therefore take up the whole armor of God, that you may be able to withstand in the evil day, and having done all to stand firm."*
> —Ephesians 6:10–13

Four Steps to Conflict Resolution

As a professional counselor, I have seen many handouts, workbooks, and even whole seminars dedicated to instructing couples about the steps to conflict resolution. I have seen everything from "10 Steps to Conflict Resolution," to suggestions to take breaks for hours and schedule a time to come back and discuss, and, in severe cases, suggestions to seek professional counseling. Although some hurts and wounds are severe enough to require outside help, I would say most conflict could be resolved much easier than most of us would think. By using biblical principles and spiritual strength from God, we can accomplish complete and healing resolution to marital conflict in four steps: stop the attack, redirect with concern for the other spouse, ask for and offer forgiveness for how you have hurt one another, and then end in prayer. An example of prayer would be that God protect you and the marriage from additional conflict and warfare from the Enemy and that He soften each of your hearts to see one another through His eyes.

1. **Stop the attack**

This is a quick and easy step: when a discussion begins to escalate and either person in the couple feels the attack, the person to realize it first should say, "We need to stop and redirect this; it is not going well and I do not want either of us to get more upset." It sounds simple enough, but staying calm enough to think of this in a heated moment is very difficult. A lot of practice and ongoing prayer asking God to spur your Spirit to do things in a Godly way, will help tremendously. With self-control and wisdom, we can choose to stop, even in the midst of being hurt or attacked. It will also take skill and talent for both individuals in the couple to actually stop when their partner requests them to; often our own anger, agenda, or pride will tempt us to keep going, but this is where we need to draw on the strength of Christ within us and have self-control and grace for our spouse.

2. **Redirect**

Once both you and your spouse have stopped arguing and throwing out insults, redirect the conversation by saying, "Tell me what about our discussion made you so upset." Then allow your spouse to tell you how they feel without interrupting them. And, to the spouse who is expressing their feelings, be respectful and keep it short. Two to three sentences should be all you need, or it will become too preachy or lengthy for your spouse to really understand and validate you. This is a reciprocal exercise called "active listening." It does not matter who starts, but both partners should have an equal opportunity to express their hurts or frustrations and then have these feelings or ideas validated by the other person by having statements repeated such as: "So what I heard you say was _____ or I see that is really hurtful to you when _____ ".

3. **Forgive**

Offering and accepting forgiveness in a relationship is the single most important thread in having a deep and lasting emotional bond. As Christians, forgiveness is the foundation of our faith. Forgiveness is the **only** reason we are "good enough" to receive eternal life in Heaven, and it is because God gave so greatly of Himself in offering Christ as payment for our sins. Imagine how much love and sacrifice that was for our Heavenly Father and His Son to do for us? Therefore, how easy should it be for us to forgive our spouse for hurtful thoughts or actions against us? The forgiveness exercise we teach our couples in marriage counseling has proven to be extremely helpful, and it is as follows: Continue on with the step of redirection from above in which you have just asked your spouse to express how they felt hurt, frustrated, or offended which caused the conflict to escalate. Then, the person listening will paraphrase what they heard their spouse say. Try to be as accurate as possible and use *their* words, not your own. The spouse that began by expressing their hurt will then give their approval as to whether they feel heard by their spouse when they paraphrased what they said. It is important that this paraphrase is to a level that makes the spouse that went first feel validated. If not the couple should start over and be calm, slow, and precise so as to not minimize the importance of being understood by one another. This step alone can be very healing and emotional, but the most important step is this: after your spouse says they feel heard and validated by you, ask him/her to forgive you for making them feel that way and express your true intention in trying to be a loving or respectful spouse to them. Then allow them to grant you forgiveness. This is crucial because it changes their heart and emotions too in actually gifting the forgiveness and allows their negative feelings to be released to God. That's why asking for and granting forgiveness is so much better than saying, "I'm sorry." When we say we are sorry, it does not involve the person whom was hurt or offended and does not offer the same level of healing. Couples will increase their communication success if they can change their language from, "I'm sorry" to "Will you please forgive me for hurting you." Once you have ensured your spouse has fully expressed themselves and forgiveness has been granted, then it is the other spouse's turn. I cannot emphasize enough that it is important that both sides are expressed, this will help the relationship feel like both spouses are being gracious and caring about one another.

4. **Pray**

Do not skip this step! You might feel better and like the conflict is over after step three, but it is healthier and in the best interest of your marriage to end a conflict in prayer. Remember the statistic I gave earlier about couples that pray together lowering their chance for divorce by 95 percent? It is very common to feel pretty good after resolving a conflict with your spouse, but then Satan drums up thoughts or feelings inside of you twenty minutes later about how you should still be hurt or offended. Asking God to protect you and your spouse from such attacks is just as important as usurping the attacks from your spouse. You can find an example prayer below. You will notice I have it written it from the viewpoint of the husband; men are the spiritual leaders of the marriage and have authority over evil on behalf of their wife and children. Both husband and wife should pray it together and stand in agreement in faith that God is the center of the relationship and the Protector of their marriage, but the husband should lead it. If there is discord in the marriage, or one spouse is stronger in faith than the other, it is still important and valuable to pray with or without the other spouse. When you took your vows at your marriage ceremony, you became "one in front of God." Therefore, either/both spouses have great spiritual authority and influence to bless and protect the other, so I encourage you to pray for each other often.

Review

- The priority in stopping the attack cycle is to step outside of our natural instincts and act out of wisdom and through our Spirit; trying to be Christ-like and pleasing to God.
- Women need to be resilient and open with our feelings even if we feel hurt, ignored, or rejected by our husbands.
- Men, try not to become hopeless, but rather do things that are loving and caring for your wives despite their emotional reaction, even if you feel personally attacked.
- Ask God for wisdom, direction, and supernatural strength to resist your human nature to be defensive and attack, and react with forgiveness in the midst of being hurt, and love in the midst of being attacked.
- Use intelligent and mature skills of resolving conflict: Stop, Redirect, Forgive, Pray.

✳ ✳ ✳

Father God,
My wife and I ask for your Godly protection in our marriage from the hurts and wounds that have occurred during conflict. May we never forget the reason we chose to marry one another. Help us to see the good intentions we have for each other, and continue to give us compassion and mercy for the ways in which each of us might be suffering physically, emotionally, or spiritually that would lead us to

treat each other poorly. Guard our hearts, wills, minds, and emotions from the attack of the Enemy, the one who will try to destroy everything that is good and worthy in our lives, especially our marriage. Give us insight and wisdom through the power of the Holy Spirit in times of disagreements that would enable each of us to hold our tongues, pray, and ask for guidance. Intercede, Lord Jesus, on our behalf in times when we feel wronged, and gently remind us of how much you sacrificed for us. Remind us that we have the strength and courage to sacrifice our own needs and offer the gift of forgiveness to our spouse. Lord, we put the health and welfare of our marriage in Your hands. Keep us on Your path, and we will always give the glory and praise to You for every good day and every blessed moment we have in our marriage. Thank You for being the one true Counselor and giving us the ultimate wisdom and knowledge in the areas in which we lack. It is only through Your grace and guidance that our marriage will succeed. We pray this in the name of Jesus.
Amen.

10

How your Wife is Like a Flower and a Hot Rod

"Let no corrupting talk come out of your mouths, but only such as is good for building up, as fits the occasion, that it may give grace to those who hear."
—Ephesians 4:29

What could a flower or a car possibly have to do with your wife? Most men I have counseled would say one of life's greatest mysteries is how to make/keep their wife happy. I hope to illustrate for husbands how they can love and care for their wives better through these two examples. By the way, I stole these analogies from my husband, through our counseling experiences; I am hoping that perhaps by giving men a mental picture it will help remind them of strategies and offer memory hooks as encouragement to them to be the **emotional caretaker** for their wife.

How is your wife like a flower? Well, most simply, because she is beautiful and delicate and she requires attention and gentle care or she will "die" emotionally and spiritually. Follow these "easy care" steps to have a gorgeous, healthy, thriving flower:

Water Your Flower

Husbands, you can start by returning to those dating/courting days: do you remember how suave you were? You would constantly tell her how beautiful she was, bought her things you know she would like, took her to new and fun places that you knew she would enjoy or that you thought might impress her? Notice how in those beginning days of your relationship you made it **all about her** and how happy it made her? Women need that. Forever. Sound like a lot of work? Not really. I will tell you right now, it is a lot easier than you think and the rewards are endless; you will have a happier wife, a more peaceful household and you will be pleasing and honoring to God. Getting to know your wife again and what is truly pleasing to her is like giving her water, to bloom, flourish, and continue to grow. Husbands, try waking up in the morning and asking yourself, "How I am going to be a blessing to my wife today? What can I do to make her day better?"

I know a lot of men are already thinking, "How can I possibly be loving, creative, or romantic every day?" Husbands, some of your ability to be creative or romantic will have to do with your temperament and how predisposed you are at being affectionate or your talent level in expressing affection in ways that are meaningful to your wife. For other men, it will depend on if you have ever seen it modeled for you; either by your parents or other respected adults in your life. Often men whom did not have a Godly role model for them when they were younger can learn a lot about how to be a loving husband from being around other Christians and seeing strong spiritual leaders set an example for them. Still some men can be overwhelmed with thinking about ways to "water their flower" every day. But there are no excuses. We have this nifty thing called Google and a plethora of amazingly written self-help books. Also, do not hesitate to turn to the mature, successful mentors in your social circle that you could reach out to for ideas. If you do not have these men or couples in your social circles, you might want to consider getting into a new circle! In this area of caring for your wife, like many things in this book, it is about seeking knowledge and wisdom, then committing with your will to continue to pursue it, and then finally applying it to your life to achieve success within your marriage. This means finding a personalized and sensible way for you, as the husband and "gardener," to be accountable daily. Make notes, set an alarm on your phone, find an accountability partner, or even recruit your kids to help you and remind you (which will be setting the example for them of how important it is to take care of Mom).

Watering your flower could look a little like this: daily compliments, a handwritten note, small to large gifts, hugs, verbal affirmations, or giving her emotional comfort as needed. Doing special tasks for her to save her time or rubbing her feet or shoulders is always a good idea. Spending quality time with her doing things she enjoys and making the conversation about her will all help to make her one beautiful flower!

This also means you will encourage your wife to pursue things in her life that help her to grow. Help her positively work towards her goals, hopes, and dreams. Encourage her to really discover what her emotional needs are and support her in getting them met. That means you might be actually fulfilling them yourself, encouraging her to be more social, inspiring her to get some of her needs met by God, or just helping her solve life's problems. Check often to see if your flower is healthy! Sometimes from an outside perspective, you can notice when she is failing to care for herself or becoming worn, tired, etc. This is an opportunity for you to offer her care and/or give her **permission** and the time to care for herself. Especially if she is a mother, but even without children, God wired women to care for others before herself. When our husband encourages us to take care of ourselves and does not make us feel bad about financial costs, time spent away from home, or the list of chores left to do and offers to care for the children, he will help a wife have healthy self-care without guilt or anxiety. And she will come back a better, happier, and more effective wife and mother. Remember the time and investment of fertilizing always comes back tenfold during "harvest." It is very evident, physically and emotionally, if a wife is well "watered" by her husband.

Give Your Flower a Lot of Light

Be positive and a spiritual leader to your wife. It can be a difficult task for a husband to come home from a long day at work and continue to be positive and attentive for his family, but guess what? God has called you to do it, and He put all the strength, courage, and ability within you to accomplish it **if** you lean on Him. If you can be positive, encouraging, and attentive to the needs of your wife and children, you will have a family that thrives and flourishes. I would say the hardest thing to do for men is to stay positive when their wife is being negative. Remember, men; it is not so much the negativity we want to perseverate on, it is the emotional validation and comfort we are looking for. So if you can stay positive, encourage her, and help her feel heard, you will be able to significantly influence your wife into a positive mood and outlook. Sometimes all a wife needs is a few minutes to vent and she feels better. Other times it might take a little longer, but if you, as her husband, can be patient and comforting, you will see the stress, worry, and negativity leave your wife and she will be a new woman just by having your love and reassurance.

Also, be her spiritual leader. Shine the light of Jesus on her daily, on her thoughts and struggles. You can do this in many different ways, but it will be through developing your skills by trial and error that you will become talented in learning when and how your efforts will affect her positively. Leave her notes of Scripture that pertain to the worries or stress she has express to you recently. Buy her a new book or devotional if she likes to read. Buy her a new worship CD if she like music, or make her a playlist of her favorite songs. Buy her tickets to see her favorite female inspirational speaker. Pray for her. Hear her talk and acknowledge her feelings **first** and then ask if you can pray for her specifically about the concerns she just shared with you. Ask God to help her in the ways you just heard her vent about. Be specific; although prayers like, "God, please bless my wife and help her in her troubles," is a nice prayer, one that specifically addresses the areas she is currently struggling with, even if it includes you, is a lot more effective and powerful: "God, please protect my wife from the stress and conflict with her coworkers. Help guide her and give her wisdom as to how to resolve this workplace issue and bless her job so it becomes one that she truly enjoys." As wives, there is nothing more powerful than a prayer from our husbands! Prayer does so many things all in one small action; it helps to reaffirm for her that you just heard what she said, it shows her you care enough to specifically pray for her needs, and it makes her feel led, taken care of, and secure in the way you will take responsibility for her and make her feel like no matter what, between you and God, she will be safe and loved.

Many men we counsel say they feel uncomfortable praying aloud or that they pray for their wife once in awhile, but not everyday. Remember, without light your precious plant might not survive the day! This area of praying for your wife is so important I would like to offer another example: A wife tells her husband she has had a really frustrating day at the office with her boss, whom she believes doesn't really likes her and might be trying to get her fired. She then came home to fighting children, dog poop on the floor, and now she is supposed to make dinner but there is no food in the house because she has been too busy to go grocery shopping.

A common prayer I have heard from men would go something like this, "God, please help my wife calm down and not be so upset. Help her deal with the kids with more patience. Help her be less emotional and see there is more to life than worrying and being stressed all the time."

Hmmm. Most of you are probably saying, "That sounds like a pretty good prayer to me." But the above prayer lacks affirmation of her feelings, and it might end up making her feel like she is failing when she already feels defeated. Rather, the "talented" husband's prayer might sound a little more like this: "God, comfort my wife in her time of trouble. I pray that she can remember in this moment how beautiful and wonderful you made her, and please reassure her she has no reason to fear losing her job or feeling like she is not good enough, because she is amazing at what she does. Please forgive our children, Lord, and that dumb dog for adding to my wife's already stressful day. I pray that You fill her up with Your supernatural peace, joy, and energy so she can get through the rest of the day. Help her to understand how much we all love and appreciate her and keep her renewed in times when we, as her family, are falling short of fulfilling her emotional needs. I am so grateful for her, God, and I pray you show her extra favor today and bless my wife for all she does for others. I could not do what she does. In Jesus's name, I pray. Amen." (And then take her out to dinner!)

Hold her hand, put your hands on her shoulders, or hold her in your arms when you pray for her. Then give her a hug and tell her you love her after the prayer. Women receive a great deal of physical security, trust, and reassurance from physical touch. If you can complete these steps and make a habit of them, I guarantee you will see the most amazing, beautiful flower thrive and grow right before your eyes.

Treat Your Wife Like a Hot Rod or a "Project Car"

There are almost as many songs and movies about cars as there are about romance. Many men enjoy watching car restoration shows on TV, NASCAR, and working on their own cars in the garage in their spare time. If you have never worked on a car yourself, try to imagine how intimately familiar you would become with a vehicle that you are rebuilding. If you are someone who enjoys working on cars, you know exactly what I am talking about. You learn every nook and cranny, every tick, click, bang, and timing within the car's inner workings. You will spend time carefully listening, repositioning and fine tuning things. Perhaps you will spend hours looking for specialty parts so that your car runs perfectly. You might even need to seek additional professional assistance if you cannot do your own painting, bodywork, or tire mounting. We have friends and family who have spent hours—even years—restoring and fine-tuning their hot rods or collectable cars. Imagine if you put that kind of time and dedication into perfecting your ability to understand and "read" your wife?

My instruction to you as husbands is to make your wife your "project car," and when you do and invest that valuable time of loving her and caring for her well, you will watch friends, family, and people within the community "oooh" and "ahhh" over her. And you will notice how that will also lead to the most beautiful and "smooth-running" marriage and family life you could have ever imagine. There are endless comparisons to how your wife is like a "project car." Know her intimately, learn to read her, listen for misfiring and malfunctions, and predict future problems and prevent them with daily maintenance. It is so important to women that it can actually become a "deal-breaker" if they are not heard, understood, and intimately known by their husbands. I have spent a lot of time trying to explain this need in creative ways to husbands that make sense to the male brain, but the message you can take from this chapter is for you to set out on a mission to be the expert on your wife. Be the expert gardener, the genius scientist, or the world-famous chef—or whatever metaphor makes sense to you—and seek to understand her inside and out and know her like she has always wished you would!

God designed women to have a heart for their husband, and that means we desire our husband to know us intimately, better than anyone else. In Genesis 3:16, God says a "woman's desire will be for her husband," and he has the power to nurture that desire or destroy it. When you are able to know her, understand her and edify her, without her **asking you** to do so, you will earn several million "bonus points" in the eyes and heart of your wife.

Review

1. Men are assigned, by God, to emotionally care for their wives.
2. Husbands, how will you be accountable in attending to your wife's emotional needs today?
3. Encourage, praise, and appreciate your wife every day for a healthy vibrant version of your spouse.
4. Be her spiritual leader.
5. Seek to know her more intimately. Every day.

✳ ✳ ✳

Dear Heavenly Father,

Help me to be the emotional caretaker of my wife. I know this is not a natural strength for me, so I need Your help. I am asking for the supernatural guidance and Your correction in times when I fall to my instincts and lack the care and attention my wife so desperately needs from me. I am willing to be corrected and adjust my will and intention to be like Yours. Help me to see her through Your eyes Lord and give me the wisdom to care for her, pursue her, and encourage her in ways that will help her be the beautiful creation You designed her to be. Please forgive me, Father God, for the ways I have been harsh with her, neglected her, or made her feel unimportant. Let her know how much I love her and thank You for this precious gift you gave me, when I married her. In honor to You and my marriage, I consciously take on the role of the emotional caregiver to my wife. I also ask that you allow my wife to see my efforts and gently correct and guide me when I am not being comforting or pleasing to her in my attempts to care for her. Thank You for this opportunity to serve her and be close to You.

In Jesus's name I pray.

Amen.

11

He Wants to Have Sex, But All She Wants to Do is Talk

"Marriage is meant to be more about your surrender than about your satisfaction. Mutual sexual surrender is the best path to sexual satisfaction!"
—Scott Means, *Journey to Surrender*

Two problem topics we often hear from couples who come to marriage counseling: women want to have better communication, and men want to have more sex.

Better Communication
Before giving concrete skills, I believe it is crucial for us to understand why communication can be so difficult. We have already discussed in this book how differently men and women think, but let's take that a step farther and talk about experiences and circumstances that change how we perceive the world around us and how our communication is affected based on those perceptions.

The Past
Psychology would tell us that the way a person perceives and interacts with his or her world has a lot to do with their past. If you were raised in a chaotic or abusive home, you will be more

likely to perceive the world as unsafe and hostile and view others as a threat; you are very likely to develop unhealthy relationships throughout life due to your past. But someone who grew up in a family and community that was safe, supportive, and loving is set up to be more confident, be more healthy, and attract positive relationships in their lifetime.

There are many childhood wounds that can significantly affect how we relate to others and even how we perceive ourselves, which, in turn, affects how we give and receive affection. If you suffer from deep soul wounds such as abuse, trauma, rejection, or abandonment, I would highly suggest you seek individual counseling before trying to work on the communication in your marriage. We need to be the healthiest we can be individually before we can expect to thrive in our ability to communicate within our relationships without the negative affects of our past interfering or skewing our ability to have healthy perceptions and interactions with our spouse.

A childhood issue that is certain to affect your marital relationship is damage caused by an unhealthy parent-child relationship. The following explanations of the value of healthy parent-child relationships should offer us insight into how we relate to the opposite sex and how it can severely affect the way we communicate with our spouse, friends, and children. It is helpful and self-improving to seek wisdom in these areas and seek healing through Christ so that our communication and perceptions can be as healthy as possible within our marriage.

Young men need to have a strong relationship with their father for several reasons. A man's self-esteem is often rooted in the approval and acceptance of their father. If they did not receive it as a child or as a young man, they will often struggle with self-esteem or feelings of being not good enough within the marital relationship. Also, it is helpful if a man has a strong role model as a father to help engrain good morals, work ethic, and an example of how to love and treat a woman well. With that being said, how many men could say that they had this kind of father, or even a father at all? This is why I believe our society is in such a desperate need of men with the ability to lead their families spiritually and men who can be resilient emotionally.

Secondarily, the parent-child relationship affects men in how they give and receive affection, and whether or not they give it in a healthy way will be determined by their relationship with their mothers. Men who did not receive the love and nurturing they needed as a child from their mother will struggle in the marital relationship. They will look to their wife to fulfill that role in unhealthy ways. A man might make his wife his idol, and he might set unreasonable expectations of her to love and care for him. Also, a young boy's understanding of the concept of being loved unconditionally is from his mother. As we discussed in the chapter about God's unconditional love for us, it is impossible to feel perfectly loved by another human being, but a mother's love can give us a glimpse into the possibility of being loved unconditionally, like God loves us. Men are not innately designed by God to become weak or distressed if they do not receive a lot of affection; men were meant to be the emotional rock that the rest of the family relies on. A husband's biblical role is to be the primary pursuer and "giver" of affection, not desperately in need to receive it. Yes, men do need to be desired, episodically pursued by their wives, and affection from his spouse and his children is always good, but if he was well-loved by his mother, this need will not lead him to dysfunction, and a lack of affection will not be a major cause of conflict within the marriage.

For young women, their sense of beauty, value, and self-worth comes from the relationship with their father. A girl that grows up with a father that makes her feel special and prized above all else in his eyes will have a strong self-esteem and confidence, and she will be more likely to seek men that are healthy (although these women need to be careful and aware that unhealthy men are attracted to their self-confidence, and it can be tempting for the "healthy girl" to want to rescue or fix the unhealthy man). The other vital role a healthy father plays for his daughter is to set the example of how a man should treat a woman. The activity of a father dating his daughter facilitates this. There are many special interactions that can happen between a father and his daughter in this "dating" process: He can show her how a man should physically protect her and look out for her. A father can talk to her in a way that makes her feel special and cherished above all else, and it gives the father an opportunity to grow close to his daughter that proves she can trust him in times that she will need his advice or support.

A girl who is well loved by her mother is given a perfect example of how to love and nurture, not only her own children some day, but also every individual throughout her life. Because we as women are already designed by God to be loving and nurturing, having a healthy mother is a good example for a young girl to see those behaviors in action, and this will stir her desire to live up to her God-given role as caregiver and nurturer. And having a mother that is respectful and submissive to her husband is a young girl's best chance in having a healthy and thriving relationship with her own husband some day.

Understanding our past issues and where our pitfalls might lie in how we relate to one another as husband and wife is essential in improving communication between spouses to heal past hurts and wounds. Again, working through more serious issues of abuse, trauma, or poor boundaries with a professional counselor is highly recommended.

Learning about yourself, having insight, and applying Godly wisdom that you have acquired through your spiritual journey are all valuable components to having better, more effective communication with your spouse. Here are a few helpful suggestions to enhance your communication skills and the depth to which you will understand and connect with one another through a common language:

1. Husbands, allow your wife to talk to you frequently and with great emotion, even if it relates to you or your actions and even if her emotions are overwhelming to you. Allowing her to vent and express her feelings and thoughts openly with you will keep the relationship close and intimate and help her always be honest with you. Openness and honesty are essential in having good communication in a relationship. Conflict, rejection, or neglect will cause a wife to withhold or deceive you of her true feelings; this will gravely affect the emotional bond between husband and wife. Examples of responses to your wife being upset or needing to vent:

    - "I hear what you are saying is _____, and that seems like it is very stressful for you. Can I pray for you?"
    - "Wow, I can't believe you have all of that to deal with. I couldn't do what you do."
    - "Is there anything I can do to help you? Come here and let me give you a hug."
    - "You are the best mom, wife, sister, and friend. I am so blessed to have you in my life."
    - "I'm sorry you have so much to do, but you really handle it well, and, with me and God on your side, I know you can stay strong and keep it up!"

2. Wives, learn the art of speaking to your husband with respect.

Express yourself with "I" statements, try not to sound accusing to your husband, and be careful to not make him feel belittled or like a failure if he does not meet your expectations. Be respectful of when your husband needs quiet time to recharge before spending time emotionally connecting with you. Try to approach him with a kind request to talk when he is ready.

3. Both husbands and wives, choose your words carefully. Our words have the power to build people up, encourage them, and bless them or they have the ability to tear them down, hurt them, and curse them. Be slow to speak, be slow to anger, and take time to pray before discussing difficult topics and always try to see your spouse through the eyes of Christ: with mercy and forgiveness. It is so much easier to hesitate in times of conflict or anger rather than try to heal and ask for forgiveness later due to ill-spoken words.

4. When you're trying to communicate back and forth with your spouse and it is your turn to listen, make an effort to **only** listen. Listen so intently that you do not formulate your own argument, a response, or an opinion in your mind. Rather, have the intention to only understand your spouse as completely as possible. Try to see and comprehend what they are trying to say from **their** point of view. A good listener cares more about what the other person has to say than what they, themselves, are going to say next.

Good communication takes skill, practice, and, most of all, good intention in caring about your spouse and that what they try to communicate to you is more important and valuable than your own agenda. Try not to allow your own thoughts or perceptions to interfere with truly listening to what your spouse is trying to express. This is a challenge, and more of a challenge for men when the communication is about feelings and emotions, as God made you the problem-solvers and analytical thinkers in this world. But to be Christ-like is to set aside your **natural instincts** and attentively care about the thoughts, feelings, and general condition of your spouse. A wife that feels she can be open, honest, and have a safe place to share her feelings and truly experience good communication with her spouse will always feel a strong emotional connection with him. This connection is the key to a happy, healthy marriage and also a smoking hot sex life.

The Sex Talk

Let's face it, ladies: if our men can learn be our code-readers and expert communicators then we have a responsibility to make great efforts in meeting **his** needs. I know, I know . . . it is the dreaded subject of **sex**. Throughout my years as a counselor, I have read many books, research articles, and attended seminars about how to have a great sex life (for professional purposes, of course!) Some of the seminars and books I have studied addressed psychological barriers, affairs, trust issues, or reasons how past trauma or abuse affect intimacy in the marital relationship. So let me be honest: at one point in my life, if I read a book written from a man's point of view or by some "super-spiritual" woman telling wives, "You should just **want** to have sex with your husband," or "it is your **wifely** duty," I would have wanted to pitch them all in the garbage! Now, because I am able to experience sex as God intended, which is thoroughly enjoyable by both husband and wife in a healthy marriage, I can safely say that those "stupid" books were right.

We can make two fairly safe generalizations about men and sex: 1. They usually have a higher physical need for sex than women because it is a physical stress relief for them. 2. It is an important way for them to feel emotionally close to their wife.

Of course, there is the argument that, based on the person's temperament, medical conditions, age, and many other factors, sometimes the wife has a higher sex drive, and it can be a stress relief for her too, but these examples are usually the minority. I would even dare to say if a man is of younger or middle-aged in life and does not have a sex drive, there is something to be explored either medically, emotionally, or spiritually. Many women, after several years of marriage and/or after the birth of children, find their sex drive slows significantly. Perhaps, due to a traumatic delivery or other medical issues, there are physical obstacles to having enjoyable sex. It is easy to start to have less and less sex with our husbands because we are tired, we are distracted, we have children in our bed, or we do not feel romantically/emotionally close to our husband and, therefore, we do not desire to have sex with him. I have done my best to address the importance of the wife's need for emotional closeness to her husband, for husbands to understand in the other chapters. This part of the chapter will explain why it is important to have a healthy sex life in order to have a Godly marriage:

1. Sex is an important component in the emotional, physical, and spiritual health of our husbands.
2. How to improve your sex life/drive if you just aren't "feeling it."
3. How to protect your sex life/satisfaction level from deteriorating.

I Like It Like That

The first reason couples might struggle with their sexual relationship is because they do not have the same sexual preferences. This means they have different temperament needs in the area of affection and therefore one will want to have sex more often than the other or one will not want to be as "wild" as the other would desire. The important realization in this "problem area" is that, as couple, you do not allow the differences to divide you. Good communication is always the key. Early on in the sexual relationship within the marriage, the couple should identify and communicate their sexual preferences and needs. How often would they like/expect to have sex, what kind of style/positions/assertiveness, how much foreplay, etc. Without having these discussions, a couple will begin to resent each other because they are not having sex often enough, too often, or the actual behaviors during sex are being extremely annoying or even damaging to one or both spouses. In fact, the two most destructive areas that affect the marital relationship are "bad" sex and poor communication.

Early in the marriage, both individuals should be communicative and attentive to their spouse's sexual preferences and mutually agree as to what is enjoyable and satisfying for both of them as a couple. As they age and their life circumstances change, this subject needs to **continue to be** addressed and the emotions behind it for each spouse. Sex is an important component in marriage and needs to be given time, attention, and resolution if there are problems. Even if it is uncomfortable or awkward, this is **not** an area to be ignored.

The second area that can interfere with a healthy sex life is sexual fears. These fears can come from childhood or early adulthood sexual abuse, sex as an adolescent, sex before marriage, pornography, promiscuity, assumptions based on how you were raised, or the way sex might have been portrayed to you in the home or in your environment. Sexual fears might come from the smallest of hurts and wounds, but without communication and vulnerability with your spouse, fears will be left to fester and cause problems in your relationship. The area of our marriage in which we can be the most honest and vulnerable with our spouse is within the sexual relationship, which is why sex can either be so emotionally bonding or emotionally damaging.

In a biblical marriage, we have to be able to forgive our spouse if they hurt us and cause us to have an emotional fear or damage within the sexual relationship. The gift of a sexual bond is from God, and it is so important and crucial in having a fulfilling marriage for **both** husband and wife. The most important step in being forgiving is to be completely honest and discuss issues when they happen. Do not allow these issues to become taboo and hold secret resentments against your spouse. Do not be fearful or self-sacrificing about your sexual needs. Trust your spouse, and discuss if a sexual situation or experience was upsetting or painful, especially if it is causing you to be fearful of having sex with your spouse.

Another issue that can affect the ease and enjoyment of a sexual relationship within marriage is embarrassment. Both men and women can be sensitive in this area, as any person can be susceptible to having poor self-esteem or a lack of confidence in the bedroom. Unfortunately, it usually does not take a significant incident to cause traumatic issues in the area of sex relating to feeling embarrassed. One bad experience can cause a lot of difficulty for the couple to regain total enjoyment of sex again. Especially having sex in a carefree way, without the reminder or fear of being embarrassed again. For a wife, feeling ashamed or embarrassed about her physical body can also severely affect the sexual relationship. I know this issue of body image often causes men to feeling like they are walking on eggshells with their wives. Husbands, be aware that your wife is constantly "under attack" in her mind by past insults, worldly beliefs, media messages, and the negative thoughts in her head that she is fat, ugly, and not good enough.

It might be easy, whether unintentionally or during times of conflict, to make comments that will hurt your spouse and cause these feelings to become worse or more significant in her mind, thereby affecting her confidence in the area of sex and her belief that she is physically appealing to her husband. Husbands and wives, it is your responsibility to be able to open up and talk about your thoughts and insecurities that cause you to feel embarrassed in relation to sex. Pursue to discover where you think or **know** these insecurities or **lies** are coming from. If necessary, you might have to seek professional counseling to overcome these beliefs. It is vital to be confident in how you see yourself and not have feelings of embarrassment with your spouse in the sexual relationship. This is an important component in having a thriving sex life in your marriage.

Common emotions when talking about sexual problems in a marriage are anger and unforgiveness. Much like we discussed with embarrassed feelings, anger and unforgiveness can happen from hurts and wounds caused in childhood, past romantic relationships, and especially circumstances and sexual experiences that have occurred within the marriage. Sometimes this anger and unforgiveness specifically relates to the sexual experiences within the relationship, but sometimes it is completely unrelated. It is so important to remember anger and unforgiveness can come from other areas of conflict in the marriage or even from past relationships. It is important to discuss these issues and how they might be affecting the sexual relationship, but frankly the solution is quite simply to forgive and move on. The sexual relationship is so important, and it is a gift from God. Sex was intended to bring two souls closer together than any other action or behavior ever could. It refers to the Scripture that states that man and wife are to become one flesh. Sex is the "sealant" to the covenant made at the wedding altar. That is why it is so damaging when it happens outside of marriage; because it is not blessed by God, it can be used to deeply hurt and wound us. It is worth putting effort into making sure you both enjoy sex and are keeping the intimacy alive in the marriage.

He's Just Being Selfish and Demanding

Because there are so many physical and emotional factors that go into a wife being ready, willing, and able to have sex with her husband, I have often heard from my friends and in my counseling office that it is selfish or demanding of a husband to want to have sex all the time. Wives will say, "Doesn't he know how tired I am? I just don't feel like it. Doesn't he realize how hard it is to have sex with him if I am not in the mood? He doesn't meet my emotional needs, so why should I meet his sexual needs?" There are a dozen more examples I could offer, but the important part of this example is that both men and women need to apply the biblical wisdom to care for the other spouse more than themselves in order to have a fulfilling marriage. If a husband is pursuing his wife in conversation, being romantic and "watering his flower," she will naturally want to have sex with him. And with good intention and motivation from Christ, a wife can overcome her own feelings, hurts, and even physical issues to be able to truly enjoy a sexual relationship with her husband, and he will cease to be demanding or selfish. Rather she will just **want** to have sex with him **often**. I specifically joined communication and sex into one chapter because it is the similar love language for men and women. If a man goes too long without having sex with his wife, he will be unhealthy. If a wife does not have affirming and validating communication with her husband, it will cause her to be sad, anxious, and resentful. Because men feel connected to their wives through the sexual relationship and women feel connected to their husbands through communication, I often give wives this challenge: if you go a week without having sex with your husband, imagine if your husband went a whole week without talking to you? This statement puts our differences in husband/wife needs into perspective a little, doesn't it? I would highly recommend the books *Under the Sheets* by Dr. Kevin Leman and *A Celebration of Sex: A Guide to Enjoying God's Gift of Sexual Intimacy* by Douglas E. Rosenau.

There are not enough pages in this book for me to address all the issues that relate to having a good sex life, but I wanted to at least plant the seed that all husbands and wives need to pursue this blessed gift. Whether you have experienced sexual trauma, medical issues, or infidelity, I would encourage each of you to seek total and complete healing through Christ. This is not an area to ignore, underestimate or give up on. A man's need for an enjoyable sex life with his wife is just as important as a wife's need for communication and emotional resolution from conflict. I would offer you the following prayer for healing:

Prayer for a Great Sex Life

The first thing to do when praying for a great sex life is to break any "soul ties" you have with anyone else. Once all the soul ties are broken you can pray that God restores the bond that ties you **only** to your spouse. Sometimes, the more abusive or difficult the past relationships were, the harder it is to break a soul tie, so do not be afraid to pray the prayer more than once until you truly feel free.

Pray this prayer for anyone you have been married to and from whom you are now divorced; anyone who has abused you physically, verbally, or sexually; or anyone with whom you have had **any** sexual contact with, including pornography. Insert their name(s) in the blanks.

Dear Lord Jesus,

I come to You right now and ask You to break the soul ties in my life. I do not want my soul to be tied to anyone else but You, Lord Jesus. I ask you to take the Sword of Your Truth, which is Your Word, and cut the ties that bind my soul to _____. I ask you to release me from any vows, covenants, oaths, promises, expectations, or exchanges between me and _____. I ask that every exchange made between our minds, wills, souls, emotions, spirits, or physical bodies will be canceled and all attachments between us will be broken. I give back to _____ right now, by the power of Your Spirit all parts of himself/herself including all the parts of his/her body, mind, soul, will, spirit, being, expectations, emotions, and circumstances that were given to or exchanged with me. I also take back to myself, right now, by the power of Your Holy Spirit, all the parts of me that were given or taken in our relationship. I claim back all parts of me, including all parts of my body, mind, soul, will, spirit, being, expectations, emotions, and circumstances. I ask You, Lord Jesus, to separate me from _____. Make me one with myself and at peace with You. I ask you to knit back together all the fragmented pieces from the hurt, rejection, and emotional damage caused by the relationship between _____, and I ask You to do the same for him/her. Thank You for setting me free to be all the person You have created and called me to be in Your glory.

Amen.

(This prayer is paraphrased and slightly modified from the *Combat Manual for Spiritual Warfare* by Marjorie Cole)

Review

- Use Spirit-guided wisdom to think outside of your perception to have better communication and meet the needs of your spouse.
- Use self-reflection to ask yourself if past relationships, current hurt, or childhood wounds are affecting how the emotions are being communicated.
- Wives need to vent; it is their safety valve so that they can continue to handle stress and manage their emotions.
- Words have a great deal of power in a relationship. Choose them wisely.
- Sex is a very important component and a gift in marriage. Do not overlook it and have it often!
- The sexual relationship completes our "wholeness" within the marriage. We need all of these elements to have a fulfilling and sustaining marriage: emotional, spiritual, and sexual relationship.

* * *

Heavenly Father,
I am now free from any bonding ties that bound my soul to anyone but You, Father God and my spouse. I now ask You to physically, emotionally, and spiritually connect me to my spouse. I acknowledge that You gave us the gift of a sexual relationship so that we might feel closer to one another than anyone else here on this earth. I am asking you to restore that heavenly gift in our marriage today. Help us to experience the sexual relationship as you intended it to be in our marriage, as a blessing and a bonding agent that will connect us body, mind, and soul as husband and

wife. I ask for forgiveness for being selfish in my needs in the sexual relationship, for stating or even thinking that I do not want to have sex with my spouse and for not placing a higher priority in our marriage of ensuring we have a thriving sex life. I want that to change. Show my spouse and me how to be the best lovers to each other we can be: attentive, loving, and satisfying. Thank You, Jesus, for caring about every aspect of our marriage and thank You for the gift of our sexual relationship.

In Jesus's name we pray.

Amen.

12

The Jesus Factor

Jesus said to him, "I am the way, and the truth, and the life.
No one comes to the Father except through me."
—John 14:6

In this chapter, I would like to acknowledge that there are probably readers who are not yet followers of Jesus. If you are one of them, I hope you are still finding this book to be helpful and insightful. I **guarantee** that if you can take all the information and wisdom in this book and apply it to your life and marriage, even if you do not have a relationship with Christ, it will improve . . . at least for a little while. The truth is that without having the supernatural power of God within you, we, as human beings, become weary of our own daily **works** and **efforts to succeed in relationships**. Relying on Jesus for our strength, hope and inspiration makes our life, our relationships, and the world around us more successful.

People have asked me over and over through the years that I've been a marriage counselor, "What would be the single most important factor in having a great marriage?" My answer: "The way to have the most successful **life** possible, which would include your marriage, would be to accept Jesus Christ as your Savior and then spend the rest of your life emulating the love and character of Jesus to others. To be loving and compassionate like Him, slow to anger and quick to forgive like Him, and most importantly a servant to others and self-sacrificing like Him.

Possessing these qualities and being able to apply them to your relationships **without** Jesus is difficult and next to impossible. What would be the motivation to have these attribute and behaviors? In hopes that the other person will respond in a way that would be rewarding to you? Thinking it will make you feel good? What if you do not get the rewards you had hoped for? Will you be able to be perseverant and continue to do good works? Unlikely. You are only human after all. Once you make the best decision of your life to make Jesus the Lord and Leader of your life (refer to prayer in chapter 5, page 67), you will receive the gift of the Holy Spirit, which will naturally motivate you, give you the attributes of Jesus, and nudge you along your spiritual journey to become more and more refined in His ways. But there is a little bit of a formula or recipe as to how to be more Christ-like in your marriage, how you parent, and how you interact in all human relationships:

Step One: The first step is to follow the first of the two most important commandments in the Bible, "Love the Lord Your God with all your heart and with all your soul and with your entire mind and with all your strength (Mark 12:30).

When you are able to understand how much God loves you and have a burning desire within you to please Him, it will literally transform how you behave around others, how you think, and how you speak. With Jesus, you will never run out of motivation. If we are not a follower of Christ or we are unsure of our faith, we tend to question how dedicated we can be to God. How much time and effort do we invest in a "being" we do not hear or see? We have so little guarantee that He will be there for us when we are in need. The answer is to pursue Him. Ferociously pursue Him with all that you are, like the Scripture says, with your mind, heart, soul, and strength. When you do this, He will reveal Himself to you and lift every worry, burden, and heartache off of you in an instant. You will see your life, loved ones, and the world through new lenses and never want to turn back.

Step Two: This step is the second of the two greatest commandments: to love your neighbor (mother, brother, wife, and children, etc.) as yourself (Mark 12:31).

Our first mission in life, after finding a relationship with God, is to love one another. A life without serving and giving love to others is very empty. A common problem that most people have is that they focus on how **they** need to be loved or cared for, rather than focusing on the first part of the commandment: to love others as yourself. God did not create a commandment to seek love from others with all your efforts, and He did this for a reason. It was to help us keep our eyes and focus on **others**. Being self-concerned always leads to feeling depressed, bitter, and anxious. Focusing on loving and serving others gives us hope, joy, and spiritual blessings that are so abundant it is impossible to explain them in words. But when you experience God's love and rewards in your life, you will understand the truth: true joy lies in serving others and pleasing Him.

Step Three: Jesus encourages us to be like Him as He became like us (Galatians 4:12).

We know as Christians that we are supposed to try to be like Jesus, but what does that **really** mean? How does that apply to marriage? Well, first we have to know what Jesus was like as a man here on earth, to truly understand how to be more like Him. I would suggest reading the gospels often and focusing on the life of Jesus and how He spoke, behaved, and sacrificed. I am not going to make an exhaustive list of Jesus's attributes here, but just remember the next time you are judging others or you are frustrated with the expectations you have for your loved ones, to take time to reflect on how Jesus would regard them. Then ask yourself, what are **you** doing to be more like **Him**? Jesus had many roles: a teacher, a leader, a healer, a counselor, a comforter, forgiver, hero, and Savior, but first and foremost, Jesus was a servant. Never forget how He laid down His life for us and how His will and needs were sacrificed over and over to serve others. When we can put our lives into that kind of perspective, His perspective, how could we not serve one another with more joy, grace, and fulfillment?

There have been many times in my life I have wept for the ways Jesus has loved me and sacrificed for me. I am so humbled in His presence. This kind of debt can never be repaid, but I am going to do everything I can to be honoring and pleasing to Him out of gratitude for what He has done for me. This can give new life, motivation, and meaning to our role within our marriage, and I pray each of you is inspired in the same way.

Gratitude

The definition of gratitude in the Webster's dictionary is "acknowledgment of having received something good from another." The Greek translation is "the giving of thanks for God's grace." The Hebrew translation is "recognizing the good that is already yours." As Christians, when we understand the depth of God's love for us and what Jesus did at the cross for us, we become overwhelmed and humbled with **gratitude**.

What a precious word. The power of having gratitude in your life, for a relationship with God and for your spouse, is priceless. I learned a long time ago that gratitude is the key to having joy and contentment in life. Being thankful to God, even in times of trouble and difficulty, will always leave a person with less stress and anxiety. So much so that this has become my life verse:

"Do not be anxious about anything, but in everything by prayer and supplication with thanksgiving let your requests be made known to God."
—Philippians 4:6

When I counsel people with depression and anxiety, one of the first homework assignments I give them is to keep a gratitude journal. Listing out an inventory of all things we **already** possess in our lives and then to give all the thanks and glory to God. This simple exercise can instantly change our mood and overall outlook in life. Here is an excerpt from my gratitude journal while writing this book:

I am grateful first to God, for downloading the wisdom found in this book into my heart and my mind and for the ability to convey it to others in ways that will help change lives and save marriages. May all of the success be out of His power and for His glory. I am so grateful to God for my husband, Scott Rothmeyer, whom God handpicked for me, knowing that we would do marriage ministry together and that we would be equally yoked in truth, biblical wisdom, and passion for marriage. I am also thankful to Scott for believing in me and for his faith in the success of this book since the very beginning.

I am ever-thankful to my parents, Jim and Mary Kay Leukam, for teaching me about God, Jesus, faith, and how to be kind and giving to others,and most of all for setting an example of perseverance and commitment in a marriage. By observing my parents, I know that no matter how tough things get, with faith and prayer, any difficult circumstance can be overcome and love can thrive again.

I am grateful for my children. God has allowed me to be a mom in many different ways, for His purpose and glory. I am thankful for Ryan and Erica Rothmeyer, Scott's children. We are a blended family and being a stepmom is **the** hardest job I have ever had, but it has taught me a lot about patience, sacrifice, and being a positive influence in the lives of hurt and defenseless children who had no choice in how their family was altered forever by divorce. After living out daily life with Ryan and Erica, I deeply understand and have experienced how divorce truly affects children first-hand and how, with Christ, they can overcome and heal. This experience has changed how I counsel children/teens of divorce forever. I am more compassionate, accepting, and full of grace for the ways they have suffered.

I am grateful for Austin Kaiser-Joly. Austin is a very special young man who came into my life at a time when I was longing to be a mother. I began dating his father just two months before he was born. After two years of dating and being engaged, Austin's father and I married, and I was his stepmother but also so much more. I was able to help raise him since he was just a few weeks old. I was there for every major event in his life and cherished every giggle, cuddle, and hug I ever received from him. I was able to continue to be in his life after his father and I divorced until he was ten years old. Now, I am here for him as a prayer intercessor and spiritual mentor, and he will always be a part of my family and my heart.

I am grateful for my beautiful daughter Alena. She is fierce with passion and has a special love for the hurting and less fortunate. She challenges me to be direct and consistent as a parent, and her heart for Jesus blows me away everyday. She has taught me so much about how to be bold and how to make self-care a priority so that I can be effective in helping others. I am anxiously awaiting the fortress of courage (the biblical meaning of her name) and strength she will become for God's people as she matures into a young woman.

I am grateful to Kelly Dykstra for introducing me to the ARNO temperament profiling system; it has radically changed how I counsel and how quickly I am able to help people find healing through understanding how God created them. I am humbled and filled with gratitude for Marjorie Cole. Marjorie was a mentor and spiritual teacher in my life. The amount of time, attention, wisdom, and love she has shared with me changed me tremendously as a counselor and a Christian and how I viewed spiritual warfare. There are so many other people I am grateful for: my sisters, Heather and Amber, for always encouraging me, making me laugh, and giving me lots of "case studies" for this book about marriage; you two are so much more than sisters, but my dearest and bestest friends. I am thankful for my best friend, Dawn Sullivan; if not for your friendship for the last twenty years, I would not be as strong-minded and self-assured. I am thankful for my mother-in-law, Betty Lokken, Dawn Byars, Donna Hunt, Amy Erickson, Mac Franssen, Laura Vollkommer, and Angie Platt for being my prayer warriors, giving me spiritual protection and guidance from the Holy Spirit in writing this book.

It is with a heart and attitude of gratitude that I approach each day to give God all the glory for the ways He has abundantly blessed me. It is with this gratitude that I fight against the dark hopelessness of this world. I pray you may also experience joy in being grateful, every day, for every breath you take.

* * *

Dear Lord,

Thank You so much for Your power, Your grace, and forgiving me of my sin, by the sacrifice of Your Son Jesus. It is a gift I never want to take for granted. It is because You loved the world so much that You gave your one and only Son to die for us, a debt that can never be repaid. Thank You for your intense love for me, that when I feel alone or afraid I can always find comfort in You. Thank You for knowing every hair on my head and keeping every tear I shed in a bottle. You are the one true Comforter and Counselor. I pray for my husband, Scott, my children, Ryan, Erica, Austin, and Alena, and for all who read this book, that they too are overwhelmed with Your love and that their own humility and gratitude for this love would motivate them to be servants to the world in Christ-like ways. I am so humbled and grateful for the gifts You have bestowed on me. I desire to always please You. Forgive me, Lord, when I fall short, and continue to bless and protect me in life so that I can serve Your kingdom fiercely, so that on that blessed day I get to meet You, You will say, "Well done, good and faithful servant."

In Jesus's name I pray,

Amen.

Appendix
Common Marriage Myths

"Respect is earned."

Our world teaches us that both men and women need and deserve respect. This might be somewhat true, as it does not feel good to be disrespected no matter what your age or gender, but respect is needed much more at the core of a man and can either build him up or tear him down. Wives, "respect your husbands" is an instruction given to us by our Heavenly Father both in Ephesians 5:23-24 and 1 Peter 3. Because we are to submit and honor our husbands in order to obey and submit to the Lord, respect is no longer contingent on behavior but is rather a command from God that if followed will only lead to grace and blessing in our individual life. In a biblical marriage, respect is freely given, not earned. Respect is given even if, **especially** if, the spouse's behaviors are not pleasing to you. God reassures us that our treasure in Heaven will be great, but the sacrifice is here on earth. In the moment, one of the most Godly things women can do is to be respectful, even when her husband is undeserving of it. It is in comparison to how we were all undeserving of Christ's sacrifice on the cross for us.

"I don't want to forgive, because I know/am afraid they will do it again!"

First of all, in Matthew 18:22 Jesus says we are to forgive seventy times seven! Secondly, what if God had that requirement with you? That would mean if we ever repeated the same sin, it would not be forgiven! Hmmm, better rethink this one, huh? If the standard for forgiveness is that our spouse should not reoffend, or should quickly learn from their mistakes, imagine when you are standing at Heaven's door and God's asks, how many times were you unkind or showed anger or overlooked the needs of the poor or . . . so on and so on. God is loving and merciful, and we are called to be the same, especially for our spouse. God gave His son, Jesus, so that we could be saved and our sins forgiven. Forgiveness is a gift freely given. Most importantly we forgive because it sets **us** free from hurt, resentment, and unwanted bondage. We can simply pass on the gift that was given to us by the price Jesus paid at the cross. This also means if we say we forgive one another at some point, our thoughts or feelings might lead us to become angry, hurt, or bitter about the same offense again. It is **our** responsibility to be healthy and well in our soul, so we will have to forgive again and again in order to receive the freedom that comes with letting go of the offense and letting go of the judgment we hold against the offender (mostly likely our spouse). This kind of freedom is better than the fear of being hurt again, because that is unavoidable, but grace (unmerited favor and forgiveness) never runs out.

"I cannot handle any more pain!"

I think one of the most helpful and well-known verse in the Bible is Philippians 4:13, "I can do all things through Him who strengthens me." The truth is, as believers, we should be leaning on God for our strengths and even amidst the worst of marital "storms" there is nothing He cannot bring you through. More importantly, there is nothing He cannot bring you out the other

side of stronger, wiser, and more deeply rooted in your relationship with Him. Trying to avoid pain or negative emotions always
leads to dysfunction in relationships, emotional issues, spiritual issues, and even physical issues. Especially when women go
through something difficult emotionally, they are not too eager to
experience those feelings again, but the consequences of running
from difficult feelings, building a wall up against feeling our own
emotions, building a wall to keep those whom have hurt us from
getting close, or stuffing them back down within us will always
cause more pain and harm in the end than if she would just hold
the hand of God and walk through the pain at the time this is
happening. You can do it!

"You should be able to trust that your spouse will not hurt you!"

Hopefully by reading this book, you can further understand that
it is not about "trust" when your spouse hurts you. It is usually
about falling to our weaknesses, either as a male or a female or in
our temperament. I have met very few people who have pure mal-
ice for their spouse. The intention of the individual is usually very
good; they love their spouse and want to do the right thing, but
under stressful circumstances or in a moment of weakness they
will lash out and cause the other spouse pain. The most important
thing we can do is to ask for forgiveness and express our **intention**, which was to **not** cause our spouse hurts or wounds. For
example: The request of a wife might be of her husband, "Please
don't bring your problems home from work and be angry with
the family because it hurts me." But for a week the husband has
been frustrated and unapproachable, and the wife is beginning to
feel frustrated that her husband cannot keep himself from hurting
her. The answer would be for the husband to say, "My intention

is to provide well for my family, but work has been slow and that makes me feels stressed and like a failure, therefore I may have been short or crabby with you lately. Will you please forgive me?" So the wife cannot expect perfection from her husband, but if he can express his intention and where the negative behavior is coming from, and then if the wife can forgive him, this is no longer a matter of trust, but rather acknowledging we are all human with a sinful nature, and we will fail each other no matter how much we love each other or how hard we try our best to gain the other spouse's trust and approval.

Now, there could be a circumstance where the spouse is truly untrustworthy. In that situation we must put our faith and trust in God. We still need to try to trust our spouse over and over and know that God will convict the spouse if they are doing wrongful things. And if it is a case of infidelity or lying, we have to trust that God will reveal it to us in time, without us having to live in fear or chaos because we cannot trust our spouse. This is not healthy. A certain level of trust between husband and wife does need to exist, but we must understand our spouse will hurt us at times, and through forgiveness trust needs to be quickly restored through faith that it is necessary to have a healthy marriage. We do not have to fear the possibility of our spouse hurting us again or breaking our trust because we are all sinners and it will happen. **Trust me**.

"Men and Women are Equal" (I can do anything he/she can do)

If you have gotten this far in the book and have not stopped reading it yet, let me see if this will do it: Men and women **are not** equal. Equal means identical, alike, one in the same. Men and women were both created in God's image and are equal in **value**

and worth in His eyes, but we each need to own the qualities at which we naturally excel and those at which we do not, while not feeling shame or guilt or allowing our natural weaknesses to cause damage in our marriage. Many people reading this book might feel offended or make strong arguments that they, as women, are more hardworking than their spouse, or that the male is more nurturing, or that the wife is more of the handyman, or the husband is a nurse and a great caregiver. Sure, there are exceptions to the generalities, and women can have successful careers and men can be great nurturing dads, but like so many things in life, until we accept who God made each of us to be, we will just never be as successful as we could be in life and in our marriage. Also, there is truth in how we will naturally accomplish feats that are our gender strengths with less stress and effort because God made us to do it naturally. This means for men and women there are some specific roles to take on: Wives, you were made to nurture, be a caregiver and servant, and be the relationship-savvy moderator in the marriage. You will know when there is unresolved conflict or hurt feelings and when they need to be discussed. Men, you were made to be the provider, protector, spiritual leader, and emotional caretaker in the marriage. You are responsible for your wife and children's physical, emotion, and spiritual well-being. When we fall into these God-given roles, we will have less stress, anxiety, and pressure in our lives, because God already gave us all the gifts, tools, and instinct to do these roles well.

"I deserve to be happy!"

In my fifteen years of counseling, I do not know how many times I have heard people say this. People will give many justifications as to how miserable they are and how it is their spouse's fault that they are so unhappy. Our society focuses too much on being "happy" and self-gratification. An interesting observation to me is that in a world that boasts of self-care and spends more time and money on "self" than ever before, people seem more miserable than ever. So spending all this time at the spa, the gym, vacations, going shopping, consuming alcohol, etc. isn't really working, is it? My answer to the statement, "I deserve to be happy" is a little harsh but true, "No, you **deserve** to go to hell, but Jesus gave up His life for you so you could have eternal life." I know it is hard to live your life with this revelation on the forefront. The daily barrage of the world, tempting us to just self-soothe from our daily stress, is a constant message through TV, social media, and daily conversation. The reality: there is little in this world that is actually fulfilling other than the love of Christ and then showing that love to others out of pure gratitude and honor to God for all He has given us. Seek to serve others, seek to be grateful and always, always give all the glory for the good in your life to God, and you will be happier than you could have ever imagined.

"I have the right to be mad."

After conflict with a spouse or even a betrayal by a friend or coworker, isn't this statement ringing loud and true in our heads? We will have a whole line of defense ready in our minds so that if at any moment we had to present it in a court of law, we would have an opening argument and lots of viable evidence to **prove** we were **wronged**. But when it comes down to it, what good is being "right" or holding on to our "rights" doing for us? Christ gave up all of His rights for you; could you perhaps give up your right to be mad? True inner peace comes through forgiveness, so there is no good for you or your soul that can come from holding on to the injustices committed against you. I have been caught in this trap many times myself; the answer is always to get in the Word and read about the character of God, the attitude of Christ, and the greater calling on my life to rise above my **feelings**. There were even times when I was writing this book that I would have conflict with my husband and then began editing a chapter, rereading God's wisdom in these pages, I truly felt convicted that I was not going to have satisfaction in holding on to the anger or my right to be mad at my husband. So, out of gratitude for God's love for me and out of a higher understanding of what brings peace and spiritual blessing in my life, I gave up my rights and chose to forgive and reconnect with my spouse. It is worth it every time, and afterwards, I usually wish I would have done it sooner.

Why should I keep trying when my spouse has treated me so poorly?

This is the biggest reason that marriages end: we are not completely submitted to God. Our own needs and desires can be unmet for a long time, and then we become bitter and resentful towards our spouse. We might even have a very legitimate argument for our emotional pain caused by our spouse. But the more we focus on how we feel, what we deserve, or grieve the life we wished we had, the more we are left feeling disappointed and defeated. The following Scripture indicates the lack of satisfaction or fulfillment in material things, but emotions and relationship needs are similar. We cannot be so covetous of the "perfect" relationship or how we believe we deserve to be treated that we sacrifice our spiritual calling to be pleasing to God. Instead, we need to focus on how to nurture our dependence on God and secure our future happiness in Heaven. When our "treasure" is Heaven bound, our earthbound needs and desires will become minor in comparison. With a passion in our heart to do God's will, we are sure to have new motivation for our role to love and sacrifice for the marriage and our spouse. And as we put forth new love, affection, and effort into our marriage, we can actually fall in love with our spouse again and perhaps in even stronger, deeper ways. To really yearn for Heaven, I think it is helpful to know what to expect, therefore I would recommend the book *Heaven* by Randy Alcorn.

Luke 12:33-34 says this:

> *"Sell your possessions and give to the poor. Provide purses for yourselves that will not wear out, a treasure in Heaven that will not be exhausted, where no thief comes near and no moth destroys. For where your treasure is, there your heart will be also."*

Additional Prayers

Prayer to Bless Your Home

Go to each room and make a sign of the cross with anointed oil over each doorway and headboards of each bed, including patio doors. You can buy anointed oil at Christian bookstores or online. Then, continue by praying:

> *"As the owners of our home, _____ (insert the owner's/ renter's full first and last name, ex. John and Sally Smith), we spiritually, physically, and emotionally claim this place for the kingdom of Jesus Christ our Lord and Savior. Victory is ours through the blood of the Lamb, and we cover this home, this doorway, and every entrance and exit with His precious and holy sacrifice in the name of Jesus Christ our Savior. We command any evil, darkness, or enemies of Jesus Christ to be bound and flee at once in the name of Jesus. With this anointed oil we pray for our Heavenly Father to always protect our home from evil and invite His holy and angelic army to shield our home and family from harm. We give praise and thanks to the Great Protector and Redeemer Jesus Christ for His blessings over our family and this home. It is in Your holy and precious light we wish to live and exist, in peace, in this home. We have complete trust in You and place this home in Your hands Father God.*
> *Amen."*

To bless the outside of your house (which is also good to do if you own a place of business), put four stakes in the ground at the edges of your property and pray,

> "We command Satan and all enemies of Christ to never cross these boundaries in the name of Jesus Christ our Lord and Savior, as we have staked and claimed this property as His, our Father God, and for the kingdom of Heaven. With the spiritual authority given to us by our Heavenly Father and through the name of Jesus, we rebuke Satan and all enemies of Christ from this land and our home and ask You, God, to cast them into the pit of Hell where they came from and command these evil spirits and all enemies of Christ to never again enter this home or property in Jesus's name. This property is now blessed and claimed for the service and obedience of our Sovereign Lord, Jesus Christ. We ask for all of these blessings and protection of our home in the name of Jesus Christ, our Lord and Redeemer.
> Amen."

Prayer for Finances

Finances are often a source of conflict in marriage. By faith, we believe God is in charge of our finances. He gives us the gifts to do our job, favor in the area of opportunities, and protection in the area of warfare against us. Part of His promise in taking care of our finances, has to do with obedience. Malachi 3:10 states that if we bring God the tithe (ten percent) of all we make, He will ensure we will always have abundance. It also states in Malachi 3:11 that He will then protect us from Satan trying to devour us. Scott and I never "cheat" God or try to short what is not rightfully ours. We always give ten percent of our earnings to our church, plus more offerings to several different ministries because we are so grateful to God for how good He is to us. The more we give, the more He blesses us; that is how our gracious Father works. When we have this Heaven mindset, there will be little in the way of stress or anxiety within the marital relationship to have conflict about, rather as a couple we can come together and simply have faith and gratitude for how good God is and how much He loves us and He will always take care of us financially, and in every way.

Father God,

We acknowledge every good thing comes from You. We believe Your Word to be truth and that if we have faith in You, You will always take care of our needs. As it says in Matthew 6:31-33, "Therefore do not worry, saying 'What shall I eat?' or 'What shall I drink?' or 'What shall I wear?' For Your Heavenly Father knows that you need all these things. But seek first the kingdom of God and His righteousness and all these things shall be added to you." God, thank You for all the ways you have blessed me and my family and I give all the glory to You for what we have. I pray that You bind us to Your financial favor in our lives, that You can trust us to be good stewards of your wealth. We will be thankful and generous to others as You share it with us. I will honor you with at least a tenth of all that I earn as a testimony of my faith and gratitude that you are the source and fountain of my wealth, spiritually and financially. Through Your generosity in our lives, we will resist having fear or stress about money or provisions and trust you. We thank You and we acknowledge financial blessing is never earned by how hard we work, but rather by Your generous and Fatherly nature. May we always remember

to trust in You for our financial security.
In Jesus's name, we pray.
Amen.